Government as Employer—Setting an Example?

P.B. Beaumont
Lecturer in Industrial Relations at the University of Glasgow

ROYAL INSTITUTE OF PUBLIC ADMINISTRATION

First published in 1981

Published by the Royal Institute of Public Administration, 3 Birdcage Walk, London SW1H 9JJ.

Printed in England by Victoria House Printing Co., 25 Cowcross Street, London EC1.

ISBN 0 900628 20 0

Foreword

This is not a general survey of industrial relations and employment practices in the civil service. Rather, it examines a quite specific argument frequently put forward in official reports and academic articles, namely that government should be a best practice employer in order to produce a harmonious, efficiently run public sector and provide an example for other employers to follow. The extent to which this principle has been put into practice in the civil service in Britain is the subject of this book.

In developing this general line of argument I acknowledge with gratitude the many helpful discussions on the subject with Professor A.W.J. Thomson at Glasgow University. A number of people in the Civil Service Department and Department of Employment kindly provided both information and comments on certain individual topics.

Because the final draft of the book was completed in early June 1980, the text does not cover any substantive discussions or changes in civil service employment practices and arrangements that occurred after that date. However, at the time of going to press, a number of important discussions were taking place on matters such as the pay settlement arrangements in the non-industrial civil service. These discussions raised issues that were consistent with, and indeed predictable on the basis of, the argument presented here. It is hoped that this book will make a timely contribution to the relatively small body of literature on the government's role as an employer.

P.B. BEAUMONT
October, 1980

Contents

Page

Foreword   5

Introduction   9

1 Recruitment of Disadvantaged Workers   15

2 Encouragement of Unionization   21

3 Terms and Conditions of Employment   27

4 Termination of Employment   51

5 Conclusions   57

Appendix I   Model Redundancy Agreement   65

Appendix II Code of Practice on Premature Retirement   69

References   75

Introduction

British government has assumed the basic roles of paymaster-overseer, buyer, protector, rulemaker, peacemaker, incomes regulator, manpower-manager and employer.[1] As government becomes a larger, direct employer of labour (as of October, 1979, there were 712,300 civil servants, of whom 552,000 were in the non-industrial civil service), tensions and conflicts between its employer function and its other roles, most notably that of incomes regulator, are likely to develop. The nature and extent of this conflict will very much depend on just what sort of employer the government is in practice.

The lack of systematic discussion of what should be, and indeed are, the nature, role and responsibilities of government as a direct employer of labour seems to derive from the belief that 'theoretical' concepts of the government's role as an employer are of relatively little help in analysing the issues and problems that face government in this role.[2]

Basic concepts

One concept of the government's role as employer that has received some attention in Britain and elsewhere is that the government may, and indeed should, by the treatment of its own employees, provide an example of 'good practice' to private sector employers and thus contribute to the attainment of certain desired social ends. Fores and Heath, for example, in their discussion of the civil service pay structure in Britain argue that:

> civil service internal decisions on pay rates and pay differentials are influential throughout a wide section of the educated community, and the significance of pay decisions in the civil service is probably much wider than the number of people employed in the home civil service would seem to indicate. If this is correct, it would appear to follow that the civil service would be in a position to exercise a dynamic purposive pay policy which could take heed of general national priorities.[3]

The authors then suggest that the civil service, as the largest single employer of scientific personnel in the country, could use its pay structure to try to stem the flow of graduates into the pure sciences at the expense of the applied sciences. A number of royal commission reports such as that in 1944-46 on the implications of introducing

9

equal pay, have referred to notions of government as a good or model employer.[4] The various royal commissions on the civil service itself have also referred at some length to these notions. The report of the Priestley Commission stated that

> there has been an extension in the practices which today would lead one to describe an employer as 'good' and that this change suggests that practical guidance can now be secured from the term. The 'good employer' is not necessarily the one who offers the highest rates of pay. He seeks rather to provide stability and continuity of employment, and consults with representatives of his employees upon changes that affect both their remuneration and their conditions of work. He provides adequate facilities for training and advancement and carries on a range of practices which today constitute good management, whether they be formalised in joint consultation along civil services lines or not. Such employers are likely to be among the more progressive in all espects of management policy ...[5]

The Commission then argued that the civil service should be a 'good' employer of labour along these lines. It is particularly important for the present study to note the Commission's description of the 'good employer' in both *substantive* and *procedural* terms.

The case for government adopting a model or good employer role can be argued on a number of grounds. First, the greater freedom of manoeuvre of the government as an employer (at least in the sense of being relatively free from profit and loss worries) allows it to take a more long-term perspective than most private sector employers. Accordingly this natural advantage should be utilized to test new practices and arrangements that the status quo-oriented private sector employer will be reluctant to adopt before their value is proven. It may be argued that government should assume such a role since it cannot reasonably expect the private sector to enthusiastically embrace government-backed 'socially progressive' measures unless government itself is prepared to introduce such measures for its own employees.

Another reason that government might act as a best practice employer is to contribute substantially to the 'efficient' operation of the civil service. By following best employment practices the government can hope to attract and retain a high quality labour force and minimize union-management difficulties and thus ensure relatively efficient provision of services. This latter argument, the one emphasised here, is well illustrated by the terms of reference of a study group set up by the Treasury in 1943 to study physical working conditions in the civil service. Their task was 'to consider how the efficiency of the Civil Service might be increased by bringing its standards of physical working conditions into conformity with the best practice in commerce and industry.'[6] This group went on to say

that their findings were being published in the hope that they would
be an influence for change among other employers.

The Priestley Commission, and indeed the earlier commissions on the
civil service, referred to *both* a model employer notion and a good
employer notion. It is therefore necessary to distinguish, at least
briefly at this stage, between these two terms. An indication of the
different shades of meaning given to the model employer notion in
wage determination terms is illustrated by the following extract from
the evidence of the Civil Service Clerical Association to the Tomlin
Commission in 1929:

> Within the experience of the Association, which goes back some
> thirty years, successive modifications have been introduced into
> this principle which cumulatively have been destructive of the
> principle itself. Thus, from conditions such as to provide an
> 'example' to private employers throughout the country — a phrase
> which implies that Service conditions should be somewhat in
> advance of the best conditions in private employment — we have
> passed in our experience to 'conditions equal to those given by the
> best employers outside the Service.' From this we have passed to
> 'conditions as good as those afforded by good outside employers.'
> At a still later stage, the criterion became as 'good as those provided
> by good outside employers, regard being had to the advantage
> enjoyed by Civil Servants in the matters of hours, sick leave,
> pensions, etc.' Finally the doctrine has become that 'the State
> should afford conditions not "out of scale" with those of outside
> industry.'[7]

On the basis of such views we broadly *define* good employer as keeping
up with the terms and conditions of employment and service (as
broadly defined by the earlier quote from the report of the Priestley
Commission) provided by the best private sector employers; the term
model employer is taken to mean the provision of terms and conditions
designed to provide an example for *all* other employers to follow.
The important distinction between the two concepts is that the model
employer notion sees the civil service as completely uninfluenced by
private sector employment practices, whereas the good employer
notion envisages a two-way relationship between the civil service and
the private sector — the government is influenced by the best private
sector employers and in turn hopes to influence by example the rest
of the private sector. It is essential to note that *the* rationale for
adopting a model employer role is the desire to influence by example
the practices of other employers, whereas in the case of the good
employer role this is not the major consideration but rather appears
to be a hoped-for, secondary effect — a bonus, albeit an important
one, coming in addition to the major benefit: the creation of an
efficient civil service. These hoped-for effects are perhaps best

illustrated by the earlier quoted reference to the study group inquiring into physical working conditions in the civil service.

Issues for examination

While the model employer concept was important in the period before extensive workforce unionization in Britain, the good employer concept is of most contemporary relevance in discussing the position of civil service employees. It appears that the government has *in principle* sought to act as a good employer in a number of ways in its treatment of civil service employees, largely on the grounds that this will avoid criticism that it is a niggardly employer and will make an important contribution to the development of an efficiently-run civil service. This book examines the available evidence to see how far this commitment has been put into practice, and notes some of the problems and objections encountered.

In addition, we ask if there is evidence to suggest that this good employer role has had any impact in influencing private sector employers (other than the best practice ones) to follow suit. Although, as we have indicated, this has not been a major factor in the government's decision to act as a good employer, it is an important potential spillover. It is a particularly important effect to examine in the context of British industrial relations where there has historically been such a strong reluctance to legislate for the establishment of best practice standards. The strong preference for 'voluntarism' in industrial relations was an important defining feature of the British system to the decade of the seventies. As Phelps Brown has said, 'When British industrial relations are compared with those of the other democracies they stand out because they are so little regulated by law'.[8] The traditional preference in Britain has always been for the voluntary adoption of such standards, but with the government trying to influence the extent and speed of the adoption process by means such as its own well-publicized treatment of civil service employees, the imposition of specific regulations on government contractors, and the issuance of codes of practice. In short, this book will look at whether the government has behaved as a good employer in its treatment of civil service employees, and, where there is evidence to this effect, whether it appears to have had any impact in raising standards in the private sector.

In seeking to answer these questions, we will examine the three sequential stages of the employment relationship: recruitment, the on-going relationship, and termination. Specifically, we will examine the employment of disadvantaged workers, the acceptance of unionization, the wage standards of employees, and the dismissal of employees for reasons of redundancy. These cases are not, however, the only ones for which it may be argued that government should act or indeed has acted as a good practice employer. For example, a recent OECD report on working life strongly urged the need for governments of member countries to assume a leadership-by-example role in relation to the quality of working life by introducing such experiments for their own employees.[9] In this regard one could point to the early adoption of flexible working hour arrangements in many civil service departments. Indeed in 1974 the Inland Revenue Staff Federation claimed that 'the Revenue now leads the whole of the United Kingdom and virtually the whole of Europe in flexible hours.' This powerful claim in fact seemed to be well founded, as, with the possible exception of Messerschmitt in Germany, no other employer of comparable size had at the time extended full flexible working hours to its staff.[10]

The analysis in this book could therefore be usefully extended and applied to a consideration of other facets of individual and collective employment relations in the civil service. The four areas selected are arguably among the most important for illustrating the potential value and difficulties of the government trying to implement the notion of a best practice employer.

We are not suggesting that this notion provides anything approaching a complete theory of government's employer role but the present study suggests that this notion does aid the understanding of certain aspects of the employment relationship in the civil service. Furthermore, it provides a useful organizational tool for constructing an analytical framework broad enough to encompass a discussion of the various influences on government as a direct employer of labour in the civil service. In short, the concept seems to have both substantive and analytical value in considering the nature of employment relationships in the civil service.

The possibility of government acting as a good employer in practice is particularly interesting in view of the fact that *in strictly legal terms* civil servants have long enjoyed fewer employment rights than their private sector counterparts in Britain. For example, until recently the protection of certain pieces of legislation (e.g., health and safety at work) was not extended to the civil service. This position has changed substantially in recent years with legislation either applying directly to the civil service, or indirectly in that government assurances have been given that the conditions applying to civil servants will not be less favourable than those legislated for other employees. The provisions of the Contracts of Employment Act 1972, the Health and Safety at Work Act 1974, the Employment Protection Act 1975, the Trade Union and Labour Relations Act 1974, the Sex Discrimination Act 1975 and the Race Relations Act 1976 are all relevant and important in this regard. More fundamentally, there has even been doubt expressed as to whether civil servants actually have a contract of employment, with the possibility of obtaining redress for unfair dismissal. Certainly where nothing is said about security of tenure, the Crown can dismiss civil servants at will. In some cases it has even been suggested that this prerogative can override the express terms of a contract of service and cannot be restricted except by statute, so that the Crown is able to ignore the terms of any agreement at its pleasure.[11] Furthermore, in 1964 when the government accepted Recommendation 119 of the International Labour Office (ILO) on unfair dismissals it did so with certain reservations, most notably that pertaining to the need to keep the ultimate right of the Crown to dismiss at will. However, if one takes into account actual practice, the above reservation was, as Wedderburn noted, certainly a strange one because dismissal procedures in civil service departments are excellent illustrations of the 'salutary effects of formal procedures in preventing arbitrary dismissal'.[12] This position in practice, as opposed to law, arguably derives from the concern of the government to act as a good practice employer in procedural terms.

Finally, except where specifically distinguished, we refer in this book to the non-industrial civil service, in particular those grades covered by the operation of the Civil Service Pay Research Unit. However, it is not always possible to provide separate figures for the industrial and non-industrial parts of the civil service. Indeed the lack of disaggregated data on certain topics means that we can only present figures for 'national government'. If this were a comprehensive examination of the industrial relations systems of the two parts of the civil service, which obviously differ in a number of important respects, this data limitation could constitute a significant constraint on our analysis. But in looking specifically at the concept of the good practice employer it is much less of a problem, in view of the applicability of the concept to both parts of the civil service. Indeed, one could argue that its applicability extends throughout the public sector; for example, the 1946 charter for the local government service stated that while local authorities should not take the lead in determining pay standards, they should be in the 'first flight of good employers'.[13] This fact is important in view of instances such as the transference of the Post Office from civil service to nationalized industry status. The value of limiting this study to the civil service stems from its position at the very heart of the public sector. In this regard it should be noted that the civil service can lead by example *within* the public sector, as was the case with the introduction of equal pay.

Chapter 1

Recruitment of Disadvantaged Workers

The merit principle, on which the civil service's official recruitment policy is based, means that all persons eligible under the national requirements should have equal opportunity for employment and advancement based on ability, qualifications, and fitness for work. It prohibits discrimination on the basis of colour, race, ethnic or national origin and applies to all departments and all grades and positions in both the industrial and non-industrial civil service. This merit-based approach is consistent with good employer practice, particularly if motivated by the desire to build an efficient civil service — the public obtains the best value for money where civil servants have obtained their positions solely on the basis of merit and ability.

Race and de facto discrimination

The operation of such a system, however, must be seen in the context of a society in which certain groups of individuals are disadvantaged in meeting merit-based criteria because of accumulated effects of past discrimination in education, employment, etc. Evidence that recruitment principles in the civil service may have had a disproportionate, adverse impact (in the sense that a considerably larger proportion of one racial group could not comply with a general condition or requirement) on the employment of certain ethnic minority groups was revealed in a study by the Tavistock Institute of Human Relations. This study which was undertaken in 1976-77 sought

> to explore the possibility of developing a system of monitoring equal opportunity in the civil service, acceptable to all interested parties, which would show clearly whether there are equal employment opportunities for various racial groups. The study was not concerned to study and report on any individual acts of discrimination; its purpose was to examine procedures such as recruitment, postings, training, promotion etc., to discover whether there is any way in which they could operate to the disadvantage of racial minorities.[1]

15

Basing its analysis primarily on the academic qualifications of candidates listed in the relevant application forms (an admittedly far from rigorous procedure) this study produced considerable evidence of discrimination against ethnic groups in the recruitment, selection and appraisal of staff in the civil service. For example, a sample of applicants to the Department of Health and Social Security in the London North Region in mid-1976 revealed that a third of the applicants were coloured, of whom 18% were offered a post compared to 54% of white applicants. Only one coloured applicant in eight was appointed. Furthermore, a higher proportion of new entrant clerical officers who were coloured possessed educational qualifications above the minimum (46%) compared to only 14% for white clerical officers. Although minimum educational qualifications were specified and constantly applied, an upper limit for the clerical officer grade was not specified. According to the researchers this meant that selectors used specific criteria for the lower limit and personal judgement for the upper limit, and it was unclear whether they were taking the highest qualified or matching qualifications. It appeared that on average coloured applicants needed higher qualifications than whites.

Similarly, an examination of the two Civil Service Commission competitions in 1975-76 revealed that 2% of Executive Officer grade applicants and 42% of applicants for Examiners in Insolvency were coloured. An objectively scored test is used for 'sifting' applications in the Executive Officer competition: 77% of the minority candidates failed the test as against 39% of the majority group. In the Examiner in Insolvency competition 19% of white applicants interviewed were offered a post as against 5% of the minority candidates. This substantial difference in success rate for Insolvency Examiners followed an earlier sift in which 42% of the minority candidates were rejected on ineligibility grounds as against 27% of the majority. Overall 11.6% of the majority candidates were offered appointments as against 3.2% of the minority candidates.

The major causes of negative impact on minority applicants appeared to be sifting the short-lists, interviewing, and the use of selection tests. Although no attempt was made to establish whether this disproportionate impact amounted to unlawful discrimination, it was clear, as the report concluded, that the government could not reasonably expect private employers to take equality of opportunity seriously if it failed to respond to these findings. Accordingly, a Joint Working Party was formed, consisting of representatives of the Civil Service Department, relevant government departments, the staff side of the National Joint Whitley Council (now the Council of Civil Service Unions), and the trade union side of the Joint Co-ordinating Committee for Government Industrial Establishments with the following terms of reference: 'Bearing in mind the policy of equal opportunity in the

16

Civil Service, to consider the implementation of this policy with particular reference to race, and to advise on methods of monitoring, taking account of the report of the Tavistock Institute of Human Relations; and to make recommendations.' The Civil and Public Services Association and the Society of Civil and Public Servants are currently pressing for a head count of all non-industrial civil servants to provide a statistical base to monitor any discrimination in recruitment, job placement, reports on individuals and promotion boards. In their view, a strict monitoring system is essential, particularly in order to provide an appropriate example to the private sector. This proposal is supported by the Commission for Racial Equality, but a number of other unions have expressed fears that it may serve to provoke racial disharmony. The government is at present reluctant to institute such a measure on the grounds of cost.

This evidence of *de facto* discrimination should not obscure the existence of an explicit equal opportunity policy which is taken seriously enough that preliminary monitoring operations of its effectiveness have been mounted. This is something that relatively few private sector firms appear to be able to claim. For example, a study of racial discrimination by the Political and Economic Planning Group reported that only 18% of employers in their survey had a policy against discrimination in recruitment, and that only 5% could mention specific steps that had been taken to carry it through. The report went on to state that

> even these figures probably overstate the level of employers' activity in this field, because there was no very rigorous test to establish the effectiveness of the steps that had been taken. In order to get closer to the actual workings of the policy, we asked informants who claimed that they had one whether they could cite particular cases where they had taken steps to carry it through. Only 7% of those who claimed to have a policy, or 1% of the total, could mention a specific instance where action had been taken.[2]

These sorts of findings help to put the results of the Tavistock study in context.

In the event that any significant changes do result from the Joint Working Party's deliberations on equal employment opportunity in the civil service, it is worth inquiring whether any *explicit mechanism* exists for transferring the resulting principles and practices in the area of race discrimination across to the private sector. In other words, does the government have some institutional means through which it can hope to improve on the basis of its own experience, equal opportunity practices in the private sector? There has been a clause in all government contracts requiring contractors to abide by the provisions of the Race Relations Act 1968 and to take all reasonable steps to ensure

17

that their employees and sub-contractors do the same. The substantive impact of this clause has, however, been minimal since contractors are not obliged to take positive steps to ensure equal opportunity, sanctions for non-compliance (if invoked at all) are the withholding of new contracts rather than the cancellation of existing ones, and no specialized, enforcement agency has been established to oversee compliance with the regulations.[3] The introduction of the new Race Relations Act in 1976 did little to eliminate these specific weaknesses. The only new standard condition of government contracts related to the new act is that contractors will provide on request to the Department of Employment such information about their employment policies and practices as the Department may reasonably require. The Department of Employment has, however, recently announced that it intends to monitor the non-discrimination clause in all government contracts, although the details of this proposed procedure have not yet been made public.[4] This proposal constitutes a sharp break with past British practice and raises the possibility of a reasonably serious administrative effort to support what has until now been little more than a statement of principle. Experience in the United States certainly indicates that monitoring and reviewing the employment records of government contractors is essential for making such contract clauses a meaningful policy instrument.[5]

Quota compliance for the disadvantaged

The merit-based recruitment policy of the civil service is, strictly speaking, incompatible with the acceptance of an obligation to employ pre-determined *quotas* of minority or disadvantaged workers to redress the accumulated effects of past discrimination in education and employment opportunity. More generally, the British government has been unwilling to incorporate such reverse discrimination or 'affirmative action' provisions in legislation. The only significant, long-standing exception to this generalization is the Disabled Persons (Employment) Act 1944, under which employers of 20 or more workers have a duty to employ a quota (currently 3%) of registered disabled persons. Failure to satisfy this quota is not an offence, but employers in this position have an additional obligation prescribed by the 1944 act: they are not to engage anyone who is not registered as disabled unless a permit to do so is first obtained from the Disablement Resettlement Officer. The provisions of this act are not in fact binding on government, but it has been agreed that civil service departments should accept at least the same responsibility as other employers and thus act as good employers. To this end, the Civil Service Department has issued a Code of Practice to all departments concerning the employment of registered disabled people. This code states that each department is regarded as a separate employer and therefore has a duty to: (i) employ the 3% quota of registered disabled staff; (ii) if below quota, not to discharge a registered disabled person without reasonable cause, and (iii) if below quota, to give preference to a disabled person over a non-disabled person if otherwise the respective merits of the candidates are fairly evenly balanced.

TABLE 1

Percentage of Registered Disabled Persons in Employment in Civil Service Departments, 1976-79

Department or Group	Percentage of Registered Disabled Persons			
	1976	1977	1978	1979
Agriculture, Fisheries and Food	2.9	2.8	2.6	2.4
Civil Service Department	1.4	1.4	1.6	1.6
Customs and Excise	1.7	1.6	1.8	1.8
Defence	2.3	2.1	1.9	1.4
Royal Ordnance Factories	2.0	1.8	1.6	1.4
Education and Science	2.0	2.4	2.4	2.2
Employment Group	3.0	2.5	2.8	2.7
Energy	1.6	1.8	1.6	1.7
Environment	1.8	1.8	1.7	1.7
Export Credits Guarantee Department	1.4	1.7	1.5	1.8
Foreign and Commonwealth Office	2.2	2.0	1.7	1.5
Health and Social Security	2.1	2.0	2.1	2.1
Home Office	0.8	0.5	0.6	0.7
Central Office of Information	2.1	2.1	1.8	1.8
Inland Revenue	1.9	1.6	1.6	1.8
Land Registry	1.8	2.4	2.3	2.2
Lord Chancellor's Office	1.6	1.4	1.5	1.6
Royal Mint	4.3	3.2	3.2	2.9 .
National Savings	2.4	2.3	2.4	2.6
Ordnance Survey	2.3	2.6	2.8	2.0
Overseas Development	2.0	2.0	1.8	1.5
Population, Census and Surveys	2.5	2.3	2.8	2.5
Stationery Office	3.0	3.0	3.0	3.1
Trade	2.1	2.0	2.1	1.9
Treasury	1.4	1.4	2.5	2.5
Scottish Office	1.8	2.2	2.0	1.7
Scottish Prison Service	0.3	0.4	0.4	0.3
Welsh Office	2.5	2.5	2.6	2.6
Other Government Departments (less than 1,000 staff)	*	2.0	2.1	1.9

Source: Relevant issues of the Department of Employment Gazette.
* Not reported.

Table 1 shows that only three departments or groups of departments in 1976, two in both 1977 and 1978 and one in 1979 achieved the 3% quota of registered disabled persons. In 1978 the Secretary of

State for Employment conceded that the figures were disappointing and promised new initiatives, but he maintained that the increasing disinclination among the disabled to apply for registration and an increasing tendency for them not to renew their registration was very largely responsible for the general failure to achieve the 3% quota figure.[6] It was in fact argued that the number of persons on the Disabled Register had fallen to such an extent (from 666,000 in 1961 to 532,000 in 1977) that if all those now registered were recruited by firms with a quota obligation the *average* level of compliance would still be only 2.2%. But even if an overall 3% compliance rate is impossible, the fact remains that only 12 departments in 1978 and 10 in 1979 of those listed in Table 1 complied with the more 'realistic' figure of 2.2%. Furthermore, the explanation by the Secretary of State does not sufficiently explain the poor compliance performance of the civil service relative to the private sector. Although only between 37%-39% of private sector employers were meeting their quota obligations during the years 1976-78[7] the fact remains that this is still a rather better performance than that revealed for the civil service in Table 1: the civil service seems to be actually lagging rather than leading the private sector with regard to the employment of registered disabled persons. This position should also be seen in the context of figures for the early 1970s which showed that the compliance rate for the public sector as a whole (although below the stipulated 3%) was above that for the private sector; in 1970, for example, the public sector figure was 2.9% and the private sector figure 2.3%, and in 1974 the relevant figures were 2.2% and 2.1% respectively. In short, while the general failure to comply with the quota obligation may be partially attributed to the falling size of the Disabled Persons Register, this explanation fails to account for the relatively poor position of the civil service where there is clearly scope for an improved performance relative to the private sector.

Chapter 2
Encouragement of Unionization

In Britain, at least since the report of the Royal Commission on Labour of 1891-94, numerous public pronouncements have been made in favour of encouraging union organization and collective bargaining arrangements. Furthermore, the government has ratified the ILO Convention 78 which obliges governments 'to encourage and promote the full development and utilization of machinery for voluntary negotiation between employers or employers' organizations and workers' organizations, with a view to the regulation of terms and conditions of employment by means of collective agreements.' However, before the 1970s there was no general legal support for union recognition in this country and the position was basically as follows:

> The State has taken little positive action in the past to encourage workers to join unions or to protect them from retaliatory action by their employers should they do so or induce others to join. The Government, it is true, encourages its own employees to belong to appropriate trade unions, and Government contractors are obliged to recognize the freedom of their workpeople to be members of trade unions. In industry at large, however, employers are still legally free to stipulate that an employee shall not join a trade union, on pain of dismissal if he does.[1]

In practice, of course, not all private sector employers have been equally opposed to union recognition and the establishment of collective bargaining arrangements. The well-established high levels of union organization and collective bargaining coverage in labour-intensive industries, for example, is arguably due in large measure to employer interest in having a union presence to help set a floor to wage competition in their industries.[2] Government is, however, surely unique in having for long positively and actively encouraged union organization among its employees.[3] This practice may be seen primarily as a means of structuring employee-management relations with a view to producing an efficient civil service, and secondarily as a means of encouraging wider acceptance of unions among employers.

21

Extent of collective bargaining

The civil service in Britain has long been characterized by relatively high levels of union organization, with membership estimated on the order of 43% as early as 1910.[4] This level of organization prior to the establishment of formal collective bargaining machinery led Clegg, Fox and Thompson to argue that the structure of civil service employment provides a natural haven for union organization.[5] The particularly important feature of civil service employment, they believed, was the concentration of employment in a small number of separate large-sized undertakings whose internal decision-making processes were highly bureaucratic in nature — a situation that virtually eliminated the possibility of individual bargaining. The sort of effect that has been alleged is illustrated by the following example:

> A clear-cut classification of functions, qualifications, remuneration and criteria of advancement permitted a high degree of standardization of conditions throughout government departments [and] the resulting isolation of a clerical class, common to the service and made up of individuals whose chances of promotion were relatively small, provided the basis for the Civil Service Clerical Association.[6]

The natural influence of this size-bureaucracy factor in favour of high levels of union organization was much enhanced following the establishment of formal collective bargaining arrangements in the civil service.[7] The present Whitley Council arrangements were accepted by the government in 1918-19 for the non-industrial civil service largely on the grounds that they could not deny to their own employees a negotiating structure which they so enthusiastically recommended for the private sector. Ironically, in view of the government's initial opposition to them, the Whitley Committee-based negotiation and consultative structures have survived and 'prospered' in the civil service through time in a way that has certainly not been the case in the private sector. In the non-industrial civil service some 70 departmental Whitley Councils and many more local level committees followed the establishment of the National Whitley Council in 1919, while the industrial civil service saw the establishment of the Joint Co-ordinating Committee for Government Industrial Establishments, four Trades Joint Councils, two departmental joint industrial councils and numerous consultative committees at local establishment level. Following the establishment of such negotiating arrangements it has been official policy to encourage employees to join unions; the civil service staff handbook, for example, in the non-industrial civil service urges all new employees to join staff organizations on the grounds that 'the existence of fully representative associations not only promotes good staff relations but is essential to effective negotiation of conditions of service.'[8] This official encouragement is not confined to the non-industrial civil service, but is general practice throughout much of the public sector in Britain.[9]

There are no continuous time series statistics showing the change in union membership in the non-industrial civil service for the period since the adoption of formal collective bargaining arrangements. A recent estimate indicates that union membership in the non-industrial civil service is in excess of 80%, compared to the private sector average of only 38.6% in 1974.[10] The civil service has been the leading sector of employment where high levels of union organization have been brought about and maintained with relatively little resort having been had to closed shop arrangements, such arrangements being traditionally viewed as incompatible with the underlying spirit of the Whitley Council arrangements.[11]

But perhaps the most distinctive feature of union organization in the civil service is just how far it extends up the hierarchy, penetrating well into the managerial and executive grades that are still largely unorganized in the private sector. For example, at the time of the Fulton Committee Report it was estimated that 90% of the administrative class were members of the Association of First Division Civil Servants which represented all grades in the class including Permanent Secretaries.[12] Table 2 lists grades of recruitment and membership of the nine unions affiliated to the National Staff Side in the non-industrial civil service in 1978.

TABLE 2

Civil Service Unions, Membership and Grades in 1978

Organization	Members	Grades
Civil and Public Services Association	202,171	Clerical, typing and data processing
Society of Civil and Public Servants	96,344	General and departmental grades
Institution of Professional Civil Servants	80,842	Professional, scientific and technical
Inland Revenue Staff Federation	68,157	Departmental
Civil Service Union	44,401	Basic or Unskilled
Prison Officers Association	21,745	
Association of Government Supervisors and Radio Officers	10,444	Radio and Stores
Association of First Division Civil Servants	4,873	Administrative
Association of Her Majesty's Inspectors of Taxes	2,486	Inspectors
	531,463	

Source: *Whitley Bulletin*, December 1978.

The most detailed study of white collar unionism in Britain estimated the extent of white collar union organization in national government in the 1960s at 83%, compared to only 12% in the manufacturing sector, a differential that constituted 'the best illustration of the importance of employer policies and practices as a factor in union growth'.[13] A further illustration of the fact that the high level of unionization and collective bargaining coverage of the civil service is not simply disproportionately concentrated among the traditionally highly organized male manual group is provided by Table 3. These figures indicate the proportions of different categories of employees working under the terms and conditions set by collective bargaining in national government in 1973 and 1978.

TABLE 3

The Percentage of Employees Working Under the Terms of Collective Agreements in National Government, 1973 and 1978

	Male Manuals		Female Manuals		Male Non-Manuals		Female Non-Manuals	
	1973	1978	1973	1978	1973	1978	1973	1978
National Government	96.4	97.6	96.7	98.8	98.9	99.2	99.2	99.5
All Industries/ Services	83.2	78.3	71.7	70.9	60.4	59.5	64.8	66.7
All Manufacturing Industries	83.9	77.5	73.7	68.6	46.2	64.8	47.0	70.0

Source: *New Earnings Survey 1973 and 1978,* Tables 110-11 and 203-4 respectively.

Table 3 indicates that, regardless of sex or broad occupational classification, substantially more employees in national government work under the terms of collective agreements than in industry as a whole or in the manufacturing sector.

The government's policy of encouraging unionization has been alleged to have significantly shaped the character of unions in the civil service, and in the public sector more generally. Prandy, for example, has suggested that, as a result of this 'hot-house' form of growth, they are 'less protest bodies than administrative unions ... [whose] ... function is not so much to challenge the system as to make it work more effectively by providing for the representation of staff opinions and reactions.'[14] The criteria underlying Blackburn's concept of 'unionateness', which is an ordinal measure of the extent to which employee-representative organizations are committed to the general operating principles and practices of trade unionism, would suggest that a number of the staff-representative bodies in the non-industrial civil service have been trade unions only to a rather limited extent.[15] For example, one of the criteria listed by Blackburn is affiliation to the TUC: many civil service unions have only recently affiliated. (The Society of Civil and Public Servants only joined in 1973, the Institution of Professional Civil Servants in 1976 and the Association of First Division Civil Servants in 1977.) These recent decisions to join the TUC are symptomatic of broader changes in the attitudes and behaviour of civil service unions that will be discussed in the next section.

Influence in the private sector — the Fair Wages Resolution

Has the government's example of encouraging unionization in the non-industrial civil service had any influence on trends and developments in the private sector? Here one can consider the impact of one specific measure, the Fair Wages Resolution, that obliges government contractors to recognize the right of employees to be union members and to receive the appropriate industry wage. The first Fair Wages Resolution of the House of Commons was passed in 1891 in the context of public concern over the sweated labour system. This resolution was superseded by a second one in 1909, which was in turn replaced by the third and final resolution of 1946. The principle underlying these resolutions was that the government has a duty to use its bargaining power as a contracting party to ensure that other employers observe at least certain minimum standards of fairness in their terms and conditions of employment. The 1946 resolution constituted the final stage in establishing a close connection between the concept of 'fair wages' and the terms and provisions of collective agreements — the outcome of the collective bargaining process became explicitly acknowledged as the relevant standard of 'fairness' to be met by the contractors' terms and conditions of employment. In other words, although the basic aim of these resolutions was to eliminate unfair wage competition among government contractors, they also sought to influence more generally the development of union organization and collective bargaining. Indeed it had been a tacit hope of many supporters of this particular policy instrument that these indirect effects would be of even greater significance than the effects of the direct objectives.[16]

There has in fact been a great deal of success claimed for the workings of these fair wages resolutions; one of Britain's most distinguished industrial relations scholars has gone so far as to claim that 'it can be said with confidence that, to some extent, it is this system of fair wages clauses which accounts for the functioning in this country of voluntary collective bargaining without legal sanctions.'[17] There are considerable difficulties in trying to fully assess the impact and value of these resolutions. One can examine the history of their enforcement record and find that the 1946 resolution has been a little-used measure; there were only 58 fair wages arbitration cases heard between 1946 and 1975. This sort of evidence may not, however, provide a sufficient basis for fully assessing their worth if their major influence has been through example, moral suasion and the harnessing of self-interest in favour of compliance. Nevertheless, the most detailed empirical study of the workings and impact of this resolution provides little support for the type of strong, positive conclusion suggested above. Specifically in relation to union recognition it was concluded that 'in the eyes of the Industrial Court and Government departments, anti-union attitudes and behaviour, even when openly exhibited, did not render employers in breach of the Fair Wages Resolution. In terms of the protection of trade union rights, clause 4 has been useless.'[18] More generally, the Resolution was seen to be influential only in the negative sense that

> By its very presence it forced the trade union movement to rely on its own strength and organization to attain its objectives. Not being able to rely on the Fair Wages Resolution, and in the knowledge that they would not receive any other help in this area, the trade unions took the hard road to self-reliant collective bargaining, independent of any legal protection or privilege through Government intervention. It is this which may be said to be the 'contribution' of the Fair Wages Resolution to collective bargaining and industrial relations in the United Kingdom.[19]

The impact of government encouragement on union organization and the establishment of collective bargaining arrangements is obvious in the civil service. This is also the case in the public sector more generally in that multi-variate analysis has shown that public sector employment status is *the* determinant of whether an employee is a union member and works under the terms of a collective agreement in Britain.[20] However, there is little obvious evidence to suggest that the government's lead in this regard has been followed to any real extent in the private sector, even among employers in direct contact with the government as contractors. Why has the Fair Wages Resolution, as an institutional means of transferring best employer practice to the private sector, been so unsuccessful? The basic reason seems to be the absence of administrative resources to seriously monitor its operation and consequently the invocation of few penalties or sanctions against offenders. In short, the explanation is similar to that given for the apparent ineffectivemess of the race discrimination clause discussed in the previous section.

Chapter 3

Terms and Conditions of Employment

The most controversial aspect of the model or good employer issue is that of wage standards. What little discussion of best employer concepts as exists in the work on the civil service in Britain has been confined exclusively to wage determination.[1] This is hardly surprising as the pay of civil servants is almost bound to be a controversial question in that 'if it can be argued that they are underpaid, the Government can be attacked as miserly and unjust, setting a poor example to other employers. On the other hand any suspicion that civil servants are overpaid would lead to criticisms of wasting the taxpayers' money.'[2]

These sorts of concerns have not been unique to Britain. Spero, in discussing the position in the United States, noted that 'the principles and standards by which government wages are set have always been matters of controversy between the supporters of the doctrine of the model employer and the supporters of the doctrine of the prevailing rate.'[3] In his view there is so much room for variation in the application of these two principles of governmental wage fixing that the distinctions between them often tend to disappear. The significance of this observation will, hopefully, be apparent in this chapter which first examines the evolution of the government's formal obligation as an employer in terms of civil service pay and then considers some evidence as to how this obligation has been implemented.

Evolution of wages principles

If we consider firstly the industrial service, our logical starting point is 1891 when the House of Commons passed the first of the three Fair Wages Resolutions which sought to ensure that employees engaged on work done under contract to government departments enjoy wages, hours and conditions of employment no less favourable than those generally established by collective bargaining in the relevant sector of industry.

The 1891 resolution was not in fact applied to the industrial civil service, but two years later the House of Commons passed a resolution which stated that 'no person in Her Majesty's Naval Establishments should be engaged at wages insufficient for proper maintenance, and that the conditions of labour as regards hours, wages, insurance against accidents, provisions for old age, sickness, etc., should be such as to afford an example to private employers throughout the country.'[4] In 1904 the Commons passed another resolution which stated 'that this House is of the opinion that the wages paid to unskilled workers in Government factories and shipyards should not be less than the standard rate of wages paid for similar work in other employments in the respective districts.'[5] The parliamentary debates on these two wage resolutions for the industrial civil service revealed substantial confusion and disagreement over the exact meaning of 'good employer' and 'model employer'. Although the two terms were frequently seen as similar and indeed were often used interchangeably, there were considerable differences of opinion over just what one or both terms actually meant. In the view of some members of Parliament, government, in order to be a good and/or model employer, simply had to pay the relevant trade union or area rate; to other members of the House one or both terms seemed to mean the provision of terms and conditions of employment which matched those of the best private sector employers; yet a third group felt that it was necessary for government to provide terms and conditions of employment which would provide an example for all other employers to follow.

The wording of the 1904 resolution was very much in line with the government's decision six years later to apply the terms of the second Fair Wages Resolution (itself passed in 1909) to its own employees in the industrial civil service. In contrast to the 1893 pronouncement of a model employer role, the decision to apply the terms of the Fair Wages Resolution to the industrial civil service was designed to ensure that the pay of these employees remained in line with that for comparable outside groups of employees. However, in defining 'fair wages' the 1909 resolution made explicit reference to the need to match the terms and conditions of employment provided by 'good' employers. The last Fair Wages Resolution, passed in 1946, omitted reference to 'good' employers, defining instead 'fair' wages as essentially collectively-bargained wages. The resulting implication that the good employer is one who accepts the role of collective bargaining is consistent with our earlier argument that the government has tried by example to encourage the acceptance of union organization and collective bargaining.

The Fair Wages Resolution continues to provide the basic principle underlying wage determination in the industrial civil service. An early report by the Prices and Incomes Board concluded that industrial civil servants had fallen behind the terms and conditions provided by comparable, outside employers due to the increasing incidence of shop floor bargaining in the private sector which opened up a substantial gap between wage *rates* and *earnings*.[6] In a later report the Board, as part of its general 'attack' on the inflationary consequences of the comparability criterion, recommended the introduction of productivity schemes so that a two-tier system of basic and supplementary rates now exists.[7] The key base rate in these calculations has been the M rate (derived from miscellaneous), taken from the unskilled male labourer rate in over 30 industries, split almost evenly between the public and private sectors.

In the non-industrial civil service the nature of the government's obligation as an employer was not explicitly enunciated or institutionalized as early as for the industrial civil service. However, the Royal Commission on the Civil Service (the Macdonnell Commission) of 1912-15 did state that 'it is an accepted principle with all parties that the Government should be a model employer.'[8] The civil service unions naturally sought to have this concept adopted as the major principle underlying the wage determination process in the non-industrial civil service. For example, the Civil Service Clerical Association argued in 1927 that 'the State cannot take its morals from below, but should set standards for itself from above, which should be an example for the private employer to follow.'[9] In accordance with this view, the staff side of the National Whitley Council argued before the Royal Commission on the Civil Service (the Tomlin Commission) of 1929-31 that 'the duty of being the model employer should not only be reaffirmed, but defined, and if possible extended into general principles which may serve as a guide in future decisions as to civil service pay.'[10] This position was very much opposed by the Treasury view that

> it would not be right to prescribe for civil servants rates of remuneration which were out of scale with standards normally obtaining amongst good employers outside the public service.... They must not be unduly high, because any such disparity ... would have the effect of elevating civil servants into a privileged class, and so of doing an injustice to the community, which *ex hypothesi*, would be worse off, and has always to foot the bill.[11]

However, in considering the Treasury evidence, one member of the Commission specifically asked, 'Have the Treasury taken into consideration that there is another point, namely that Government departments are supposed to lead the country on the question of salaries and wages, and that therefore the Government is in a sense bound to set a standard which the outside world takes?'[12] The response to this question by the Treasury was

> The view which the Government has taken cannot, I think, be described quite in the terms you have used; it is rather that the

Government set out to be a good or, indeed, a model employer, and by that is meant that the Government would not prescribe terms of employment which compare unfavourably with those obtaining outside the Civil Service amongst good employers.[13]

It was in fact the Treasury position which appeared to prevail with the Tomlin Commission who rejected the staff side argument in favour of the model employer notion on the grounds that 'a phrase which lends itself to such varied and contradictory interpretations affords no practical guidance for fixing wages or for indicating the responsibilities of the state towards its employees.'[14]

In the years which followed the report of the Tomlin Commission, the government deliberately sought to avoid the role of model employer whose provision of terms and conditions of employment in the non-industrial civil service would provide a lead for the private sector to follow. The government did not want to lay itself open to criticism for creating a privileged class of employees. This concern was clearly evident in the various attempts to delay union demands for the introduction of equal pay in the civil service. For example, in 1935 the Prime Minister, Stanley Baldwin, indicated the Government's fears about 'prematurely' introducing equal pay in the civil service in the following terms:

> What we have to consider today is whether or not this is the time to make another very considerable advance, placing the Civil Service still further ahead of the current practice in the country as a whole.... I do not feel that we should be acting wisely in the long run if we were to attempt to establish for this service as a whole, or for any part of it, whether divided by sex or otherwise, conditions much more favourable than those obtaining in the country as a whole so as to call for criticism on the part of the general public.[15]

It was two decades later that the Chancellor of the Exchequer informed a deputation of the National Whitley Council (in May 1954) that he was willing to authorize negotiations to institute an agreed scheme for the introduction of equal pay. A scheme was subsequently worked out which provided for equal pay to be introduced into the non-industrial civil service in stages over a seven-year period and to be fully operational by 1961. And as Kahn pointed out, 'Most other public services have followed the Treasury lead — an indication of the leading role played by the Service in the sphere of salary determination.'[16]

The arguments for and against government action as a model employer in salary terms, as presented in the Tomlin Commission report and subsequent discussions, can be placed in context by the findings of a study by Routh.[17] This study concluded that virtually all the civil service groups examined were receiving lower *real* rates in 1950 than in 1935, and indeed the majority were receiving lower real rates in 1950 than in 1895, the latter period showing a rise of over 60% in general wage rates and a rise of over 20% in national income per occupied person.

These salary trends form something of the immediate background to the establishment of the Royal Commission on the Civil Service (the Priestley Commission) of 1953-55. The report of the Priestley Commission reaffirmed the rejection of a model employer role on the grounds that 'if changes were proposed in the Civil Service with the intention of giving a lead on such matters to the country as a whole in order to further a political or social objective, Civil Service pay negotiations would become involved with political issues.'[18] This point was specifically emphasised in response to the argument of the Institution of Professional Civil Servants that the government, as the largest single employer of research workers, should give the lead in raising the pay position of scientists in the national wage hierarchy.[19] However, as we noted in the introductory section, the Priestley Commission did impose on government an obligation to act as a 'good employer' in the sense of keeping up with the terms and conditions provided by the best outside employers. In this regard the report specifically stated:

We consider that the Civil Service should be a good employer in the sense that while it should not be among those who offer the highest rates of remuneration, it should be among those who pay somewhat above the average. Expressing the point in statistical terms we should say that if it were possible to obtain for any specific job a set of rates representative of the community as a whole which could be arranged in order from top to bottom ... the Civil Service rate should not be lower than the median but not above the upper quartile.[20]

For specific criteria of wage determination, the Priestley Commission essentially followed the Tomlin Commission in recommending that use be made of outside comparisons for setting civil service pay. The real innovative feature of Priestley lay in its recommendations for the establishment of an independent fact-finding body, the Civil Service Pay Research Unit. Such a body was seen as essential because of the difficulties which had arisen because 'associations seek comparisons among what they consider to be the "better" employers, while the Treasury ... wish to include a wider range.'[21] The Commission provided a number of guidelines for the operation of the Civil Service Pay Research Unit among which was a specific rejection of the Treasury view that the civil service rate should be in harmony with the rates paid by a representative selection of employers for comparable jobs. The Commission argued instead that, as government was to be a good employer, the outside employers chosen for comparison purposes should not be representative of the employer community at large, but rather should be drawn exclusively from good outside employers.[22]

Implementation issues – favouring the civil service?

There was now an explicit set of principles guiding the government's salary obligations towards the non-industrial civil service, but problems of 'satisfactorily' implementing these obligations have inevitably remained. 'Inevitably' is deliberate – *any* system of wage comparability cannot be a straightforward, mechanical exercise free of considerable elements of discretion in matters such as the choice of particular comparisons and the extent of adjustments for non-wage differences. This discretionary element in the comparability exercise has predictably given rise to much debate among the parties concerned, as well as outsiders, about the resulting outcomes.[23] Such debates have certainly surrounded the operation of comparability-based pay systems for civil servants in a number of countries, as is illustrated by the following comment on the position in Canada:

> While the general principle of fair comparison is endorsed by unions and employers alike, no consensus has yet emerged in Canada on its interpretation and application. The unions maintain that a public employer should be the best employer, that its wage policy should be based on the highest rates being paid for comparable work in the private sector. Some even argue that Governments should assume the lead, that they should pay higher rates than the best employers in the private sector because of the essential nature of many public services, the restrictions on the use of the strike as a bargaining weapon in the public sector, and the desirability of raising basic standards by setting an example. Most Governments on the other hand have favoured a comparison with the 'average' outside employer, or even with those who pay slightly above the average. The federal Government in particular has maintained that anything more would be inflationary, thus incompatible with its overriding responsibility for the economy as a whole.[24]

The similarity of these issues with those raised in Britain will become apparent as we review below the arguments surrounding the operation of the Civil Service Pay Research Unit.

There have in fact been two quite different views of just how the Priestley Commission's recommendations have been applied. The essence of the first view is that in practice government has not merely acted as a good employer, but rather has acted as a model employer in providing terms and conditions substantially in excess of those provided by the best outside employers. Those who subscribe to this view have essentially argued that certain technical shortcomings in the application of the comparability principle have built an *upward bias* into the procedure for setting civil service terms and conditions,[25] with the result that there will be a sizeable, differential wage return to civil service employees, *ceteris paribus*. The major, *alleged*, shortcomings of the comparability setting process are: (i) biases associated with the measure of compensation used, and (ii) biases associated with the scope of the survey universe.[26]

The first category of bias contains the argument that, although comparability surveys conducted by the Civil Service Pay Research Unit do collect information on the non-pecuniary aspects of employment, the relatively favourable position of civil servants in such matters has been consistently undervalued when making the appropriate wage adjustments. The position of civil servants is seen almost exclusively in terms of pension arrangements, with relatively little recognition of the possibility that civil servants may be much less well placed in relation to other components of the fringe benefit package.[27] This point should continually be borne in mind in the following discussion of the highly controversial pension arrangements of civil servants.

The Government Actuary's Survey of Pension Schemes in 1975 found that only 39% of private sector employees were covered by occupation pension schemes, compared to 75% for the public sector as a whole and 97% of employees in the civil service.[28] In addition to this high rate of coverage it has been widely contended that the benefits of civil service pensions are substantially superior to those elsewhere. The actuary's Survey revealed, for example, that fully 63% of employees in central government were covered by *noncontributory* pension arrangements, compared to only 18% for the private sector as a whole and 21% for the public sector as a whole.[29] These sorts of differences are recognized in the pay research procedure by reducing all civil service pay rates by superannuation contributions, this reduction typically being 5%-6%.[30] Many commentators believe, however, that the size of this reduction is insufficient to offset the value of non-contributory arrangements.

But undoubtedly the most controversial aspect of civil service pension arrangements is evidenced by the following finding:

It seems that in 1975 virtually all public sector pensioners and probably more than four-fifths of private sector pensioners were receiving pensions which were being increased to a greater or lesser extent. *In the public sector the increases generally automatically followed the cost of living, under the Pensions (Increase) Acts arrangements, but relatively few private sector schemes followed closely the cost of living ...*[31]

33

These index-linked pension arrangements have figured prominently in the argument that the procedure for setting wages tends to substantially 'undervalue' the favourable non-pecuniary benefits of civil servants. In 1979 the Government Actuary undertook a review of the extent to which the superannuation benefits of civil servants are, on average, more valuable than those in comparable employment. The purpose of this exercise was to calculate 'the deduction' whose effect is to withhold from the pay of civil servants an amount of money equivalent to the extra superannuation benefits they may expect to receive in the future in respect of their present service, as compared to those to be received by their outside analogues. This deduction had been 1.75% prior to 1979, but the new review suggested that this should be raised to 2.6%.[32] However, a number of outside commentators suggested that this was still too low and that the appropriate 'deflator' should be as high as 10%.[33] The present Government has stated that the valuation of pensions in determining civil service pay is to be subject to independent outside scrutiny.[34] Furthermore, the Government, as part of its programme to cut public expenditure, is likely to review the whole issue of index-linked pensions in the public sector whose costs have risen from some £40 million in 1972 to nearly £300 million in 1979.[35] (This matter is taken up again in the concluding chapter of this book.)

The second major category of alleged technical weakness in the application of the comparability process concerns the nature of the survey universe. The first argument under this heading is that comparisons made *within* the public sector may be a potential source of upward bias in the wage determination process, via some sort of internal (to the public sector) wage round effect. The Priestley Commission did in fact suggest that comparable, good employers for the civil service should be drawn from public, semi-public as well as private employment.[36] Examination of the industrial distribution of the 253 outside organizations included in the Civil Service Pay Research Unit's 1978 Survey suggests that 36% of the 458 comparability reports came from broad industrial groupings containing a substantial public sector component.[37] Although there has been no detailed examination of the wage-setting implications of such intra-public sector comparisons, one example of the sort of effect being generally alleged may be noted. The Pay Board recommended London weighting allowances of £400 and £200 in 1974, but the civil service received allowances of £410 and £260 which the Civil Service Department said 'reflected improvements over the Pay Board's recommendations comparable to those which had already been granted in local authority fields to manuals, non-manuals and teachers.'[38] This sort of selective use of comparisons within the public sector is obviously suggestive of the effects alleged, although we have no way of knowing

34

whether this particular example is representative. The fear of this type of effect could have been important in, for example, the Pay Board's 1974 decision to reject the claim of the Institution of Professional Civil Servants that salaries for the scientific class should be determined solely by internal comparisons with professional and technical staff.[39]

However, the most common argument under this sub-heading of technical bias concerns an allegedly substantial under-representation of small-sized firms in the comparability survey. This criticism is typified by the following editorial from *The Times*:

It is bad enough that civil servants themselves decide which jobs in industry and commerce are analogous to those in the Civil Service. It is worse that they draw their comparisons solely from those firms which are closest in structure to the Civil Service, i.e.,

TABLE 4

Analysis of Organizations by Pay Research Survey and the Size of Total Workforce (%)

Survey	Total Number of Employees ('000s)					
	Under 2	2-5	5-10	10-25	25-50	Over 50
Administrative Group (Middle and Higher Grades)	2.4	21.4	28.6	14.3	16.7	16.7
Administrative Group (Clerical Grades)	3.9	13.7	29.4	27.5	13.7	11.8
Cleaners	28.0	20.0	12.0	12.0	8.0	20.0
Data Processing Category	3.9	17.7	17.7	25.5	19.6	15.7
Instructional Officer Grade III	40.0	8.0	8.0	12.0	8.0	24.0
Laboratory Attendants	5.0	35.0	10.0	20.0	10.0	20.0
Messenger and Paper-keeper Grades	24.0	16.0	16.0	4.0	12.0	28.0
Process and General Supervisory Grades	33.3	25.0	19.4	11.1	2.8	8.3
Professional and Technology Group	33.3	10.7	10.7	10.7	16.0	18.7
Radio Technicians	26.7	6.7	20.0	13.3	13.3	20.0
Secretarial Category	16.1	23.2	19.6	17.9	10.7	12.5
Telecommunications Technical Officers	26.7	13.3	20.0	13.3	13.3	13.3
Teleprinter Operating Grades	31.8	—	31.8	4.6	13.6	18.2

Source: *Report of the Civil Service Pay Research Unit Board and the Civil Service Pay Research Unit,* London. (HMSO, 1979), Appendix 8, p.55.

companies like ICI, Shell, BP, Unilever, and the big banks and insurance companies. These are inevitably also the best paid. British civil servants thus enjoy a ratchet system which in normal times ensures that their salaries are linked to those in the most efficient sectors of British industry and commerce — even though they work, generally speaking, in more congenial and less hazardous circumstances, and are much less accountable for the results of their decisions than businessmen.[40]

This editorial went on to urge that the Civil Service Pay Research Unit should take account of a wider spectrum of outside employers, in particular some of the lower-paying, smaller firms, in order to remove the present upward bias in the setting of civil service wages. The Unit has undoubtedly tended to concentrate on the larger organizations, a practice that was in fact recommended by the Priestley Commission on the grounds that 'so far as private industry and commerce are concerned, it seems likely that, although the smaller undertakings cannot be ignored, more guidance will be obtained from the larger undertakings in which, because of their size, the structure and method of grading jobs approach closer to civil service practice than do those of smaller firms.'[41] This concentration on comparisons with larger establishments is evidenced by figures for the size distribution of organizations included in the Pay Research Unit's 1978 survey which are set out in Table 4.

There is some obvious variation according to occupation, but the figures indicate a generally disproportionate concentration on larger establishments in the comparability surveys. Indeed the overall figures reveal the following position:

Employees	%
Less than 2,000	19.7
2-5,000	16.6
5-10,000	18.8
10-25,000	15.5
25-50,000	12.9
More than 50,000	16.6

The largest single group is at the bottom end of the range, but an organization employing 2,000 employees is hardly a small employer. In view of the widely-held belief in a positive correlation between pay and the size of the employment unit, these figures may indicate the existence of an upward bias in the civil service pay determination process.[42] However, the Civil Service Pay Research Unit Board concluded, on the basis of the 1978 pay research exercise, that they were 'satisfied that the methods of survey developed by the Pay Research Unit provide the best basis for the acquisition of a representative picture of the remuneration paid outside the civil service for broadly comparable work', although they did state that 'we will investigate further the likely effects of including more smaller organizations in the external survey fields.'[43]

In the United States a methodology for investigating the issue of upward bias has been established. The results there suggest considerable upward bias in the comparability-based process of wage determination for federal government employees who enjoy a sizeable wage differential over similarly qualified and experienced workers in the private sector.[44] This finding is suggestive of results that may well be found in Britain because *a priori* there seems more potential for an upward bias in the British system than in the American. The US survey expressly precludes intra-public sector comparisons and has a stipulated minimum size of survey establishment which appears to be considerably below the size range indicated in Table 4.[45] The only comparable British study to those in the United States suggested, if anything, a positive wage return to public sector employment status.[46] But in the absence of a specific investigation of the civil service, the argument of upward bias, however intuitively appealing, remains as yet unproven.

Incomes policy and the civil service

This line of argument must, however, be placed alongside the increasing claim of the civil service unions, and indeed of unions in the public sector in general, that their relative pay position has worsened through time due to their bearing a disproportionate burden of wage restraint imposed under various government incomes policies since the early 1960s. The essence of this argument is that *if* a positive wage return ever existed to civil servants (a possibility that the civil service unions would presumably deny from the outset) then its size has been steadily reduced through time under the operation of incomes policies. The basic contention of the civil service unions here, which has been supported by a number of academic commentators, is that government has 'dishonoured' its good employer obligation by attempting to enforce the terms and conditions of incomes policy most strictly on civil services.[47]

Government *might* choose to follow such an approach for several reasons. First, the size of the public sector wage bill (some 32% of all income from employment in 1974 for example) means that any induced restraint in public sector settlements may have a considerable direct effect on the level of wage costs in the economy. Secondly, wage restraint may be most practicable and feasible in the civil service, and the public sector in general, where large, centralized bargaining

37

units reduce the likelihood of local level wage 'drift' offsetting any induced restraint at the national negotiating level. Finally, any hope of encouraging restraint in the private sector may be seen to rest on the government setting a good example by first getting its own house in order. As indicated in our introductory chapter, this latter argument is one of the basic reasons for adopting a model employer role, and thus suggests that this notion, *strictly interpreted*, may (at least from the point of view of civil service employees) be *double-edged* in terms of its treatment implications: civil servants enjoy relative gains in good times but may suffer disproportionate losses in 'bad' times. As a consequence, the operation of an incomes policy increases the likelihood of a sharp clash between government's responsibilities to the country *qua* government and its duties vis-à-vis its staffs *qua* good employer.[48] This potential conflict is expressed by the then Chancellor, Selwyn Lloyd, replying to parliamentary criticism of discrimination against public sector employees during the pay pause of 1961-62: 'The Government has two sets of responsibilities. First, they have their responsibilities as employers, and secondly, those as trustees for the community as a whole and as guardian of the national interest. Of these two sets of responsibilities the second must prevail.'[49] In view of this sort of attitude and position it is not hard to understand why the civil service unions currently number among the leading opponents of incomes policies.

There is some general evidence of disproportionate concentration on public sector wage settlements during periods of incomes policy. For example, a comprehensive survey of the wage references to the Labour Government's Prices and Incomes Board for 1965-70 revealed that, while 45% of the overall workforce was covered by these references, 'its most notable bias or focus was towards the public sector — 66% of workers in the public sector were the subject of a reference to the Board at one time or another.'[50] Indeed some of these policy episodes, most notably the pay pause (1961-62) and the 'N-1' period (1971-72) have been quite explicitly aimed at the public sector. This sort of close attention to public sector settlements does not, however, indicate that public sector employees have necessarily borne a disproportionate burden of *actual* wage restraint. Indeed, this would be unlikely in view of the heterogeneous nature of incomes policies in Britain, which is illustrated by Table 5.

Some evidence, for example, suggests that the attempt to induce voluntary de-escalation of public sector settlements during 1970-72 may have been counter-productive.[51] Hawkesworth, on the basis of his findings for 1970-72 and 1974-75, concluded that *non-statutory* incomes policies have actually tended to work to the advantage of public sector employees.[52] Although identifying a similar earnings shift in favour of the public sector during 1970-72 and 1974-75, Dean was inclined to

TABLE 5

Incomes Policies, 1961-1977

Policy Period	Pay Restrictions	Implementation	Exceptions
1961-62	Zero norm	Voluntary	Existing commitments honoured
1962-63	2-2½% then 3-3½%	Voluntary	(i) 'Exceptional' productivity (ii) Labour mobility (iii) Certain differential adjustment in the national interest
1965-66	3-3½%	Voluntary	As above plus provisions for low pay
1966-67	Freeze for 6 months Zero norm	Compulsory for freeze	
1967-68	Zero norm	Voluntary but with powers of delay	(i) to (iv) of Stage 1 above
1968-69	Zero norm	Voluntary but with powers of delay	3½% average increase as a ceiling for exceptional cases. No ceiling on productivity bargaining; wage differentials and low paid workers
1969-70	2½-4½%	Voluntary but with powers of delay	As above, but no 3½% ceiling
1971-72	(n-l) policy	Voluntary, Govt. example — public sector	None
1972-73	Freeze	Compulsory	None
1973	£1-4% (12 months rule)	Compulsory	Settlements deferred by freeze Moves to equal pay
1973-74	7% or £2.25 + threshold payments	Compulsory	1% margin to deal with pay structures 'Genuine' productivity schemes Premiums for 'unsocial' hours
Social Contract	Compensation for prices changes between main settlements	Voluntary	Low pay Elimination of discrimination, particularly against women
1975-76	£6 maximum (12 months rule)	Voluntary	Equal pay
1976-77	5% with min. = £2.50 max. = £4.00	Voluntary	None

Source: S.G.B. Henry and P.A. Ormerod, 'Incomes Policy and Wage Inflation: Empirical Evidence for the U.K. 1961-77', *National Institute Economic Review*, August 1978, p.32.

attribute it to the relative insulation of the public sector wage determination process from the wage-depressing effects of rising unemployment during these years.[53] In the case of *statutory-based* incomes policy, Dean and Hawkesworth reached quite different conclusions about effects on the public sector, although they did not use the same earnings series in their calculations and did not examine precisely the same periods of time. Hawkesworth claimed that in the two statutory policy periods April 1968 to March 1970 and Autumn 1972 to Autumn 1974 public sector earnings appeared to have been more restrained than private sector earnings.[54] In contrast, Dean's examination of the two periods when incomes policy was thought to have been seriously pursued, 1965-67 and November 1972 to July 1974, led him to conclude that there had been no tendency for the relative pay of the public sector to either rise or fall.[55]

However, neither of these studies fully answered the question of whether public sector employees have borne a disproportionate burden of wage restraint. Neither made an attempt to isolate the independent effect of incomes policy on public sector earnings by controlling statistically for other possible influences on relative earnings during their periods of study. The absence of statistical controls means that the question of whether public sector earnings would have risen at a faster or slower rate in the absence of the policy cannot be answered. The findings of these two studies, then, even where they are in agreement, can only be termed suggestive, not conclusive.

The usual contentions advanced in support of the claim that public sector employees have borne a disproportionate burden of actual wage restraint are that they have received a more than proportionate share of near-norm, below average wage increases, have had only limited ability to take advantage of the special exceptions clauses (most notably productivity bargaining) to the general upper limits on pay increases imposed under these policies, and have experienced a longer time interval between settlements than was customary in the private sector. The latter argument has been particularly strongly put by the civil service unions. Their argument has been that the comparability wage-setting mechanism inevitably involves time lags, and the problems created by these lags have been substantially compounded by the tendency of incomes policies to freeze the pay structure at a particular point in time. This time-lag issue deserves further comment.

In the immediate post-Priestley years, the Civil Service Pay Research Unit surveyed the main classes of the non-industrial civil service every five years, but in 1964 the survey cycle was reduced to four years. Nevertheless, persistent delays in the completion of surveys resulted in the Unit's findings often reaching the parties after the intended dates for implementing the recommended wage increases. These delays, in conjunction with the considerable amount of time frequently spent on negotiation, meant that many civil service settlements involved substantial elements of backpay. This problem led the Labour Government during the incomes policy standstill of 1966 to stipulate that in future no more than six months' retrospection should be permitted in any civil service pay increase. Following this announcement, the survey cycle of the Pay Research Unit was reduced to three years in 1967, and then to two years in 1971. But despite these reductions in the length of the survey cycle, many civil service unions remained highly critical of various aspects of the timing. These criticisms came to a head when some 400,000 non-industrial civil servants due for a pay review in January 1973 were caught out by the imposition of the Conservative Government's incomes policy standstill. In considering the case for granting the non-industrial civil service a special wage increase under the anomalies provision of this policy, the Pay Board devoted considerable attention to the wider question of the compatibility of the pay research system with the needs and pressures of a continuing incomes policy. The view of the Pay Board was that

> although the pay research system is intended to ensure that the pay of civil servants is determined by the pay for comparable outside employments, the nature of the system is such that the pay of civil servants inevitably lags behind. Civil servants normally have to wait two years before they can catch up to the full extent permitted by the system although they receive interim increases in intermediate years.... They cannot attempt to change the timing to their advantage.[56]

The report went on to suggest certain possible reforms to the pay research system, notably the use of an annual survey cycle and the involvement of outside interests in the survey procedure. But even with these changes the Board still expressed serious doubts about the compatibility of the basic structure of civil service pay determination with the needs and pressures of a continuing incomes policy. These views were influential in the new pay formula for civil servants which was initiated in 1975 in an attempt to avoid large periodic catch-up wage increases. This new formula involved two important changes: the introduction of an annual pay research cycle and provision for wage information gathered by the Pay Research Unit to be updated between the date of reporting and the date of settlement. The settlement for non-industrial civil servants in 1975 involved an increase of 32.5% which was held to be justified on catch-up grounds, although its size was undoubtedly an embarrassment to a Government committed at the time to a policy of wage restraint. The whole system of pay research was in fact suspended in 1976 as part of the incomes policy in operation at the time, and its reintroduction in 1978 (as preparation for an April 1979 settlement) incorporated yet another set of structural changes, most notably the establishment of the Pay Research Unit Board whose basic function was to make the survey aspect of the wage determination process more independent and open to public scrutiny.

TABLE 6
Administrative, Executive and Clerical Pay

Grade	% 1956-58	% 1958-64	% 1964-68	% 1968-71	% 1971-72	% 1956-72
Assistant Secretary	26.4	28.4	15.1	27.3	7.0	174.6
Principal Exec. Officer	27.65	26.7	30.26		7.0	209.6
Senior Principal (SCEO)	29.1	24.5	21.2	30.0	7.0	171.4
Principal	22.4	24.7	18.1	28.46	7.0	147.8
Chief Exec. Officer	22.6	27.3	21.4	29.4	7.0	162.3
Senior Exec. Officer	21.1	25.0	20.9	25.0	7.0	144.7
Higher Exec. Officer	15.3	27.3	20.0	25.0	7.0	135.5
Executive Officer	13.9	22.5	18.4	24.2	7.5	120.5
Age 25	21.5	23.1	21.5	22.7	7.5	139.9
Plus extra increment				28.2	7.5	
Clerical Officer	14.2	22.2	17.6	25.9	7.5	122.2
Wages Index (End of Month)	10.6	20.1	18.9	28.6	12.4	128.2

Scientific Civil Service Pay

Grade	% 1956-58	% 1958-61	% 1961-64	% 1964-68	% 1968-71	% 1971-72	% 1956-72
Principal Scientific Officer	22.4	0.0	24.7	18.1	19.7	7.0	130.9
Senior Scientific Officer	21.8	0.0	26.5	17.9	37.2	7.0	166.9
Scientific Officer	14.6	0.0	25.1	18.4	9.2	7.5	99.3

Scientific Civil Service Pay

Grade	% 1956-58	% 1958-61	% 1961-64	% 1964-68	% 1968-71	% 1971-72	% 1956-72
Chief Experimental Officer	22.6	0.0	27.3	21.4	20.6	7.0	144.4
Senior Experimental Officer	21.1	0.0	25.0	20.9	19.7	7.0	134.2
Experimental Officer	16.3	0.0	25.9	18.0	23.0	7.0	127.6
Assistant Experimental Officer	21.2	0.0	22.8	19.4	37.2	7.5	162.0
Senior Scientific Assistant	12.4	0.0	22.0	22.9	21.8	7.5	120.9
Scientific Assistant	13.0	12.2	17.9	19.6	26.8	7.5	143.9
Wages Index	10.6	6.6	12.6	18.9	28.7	12.4	128.2

Professional and Technical Pay

Grade	% 1956-58	% 1958-65	% 1965-69	% 1969-71	% 1971-72	% 1956-72
Senior Grade	21.1	30.4	20.8	16.0	13.1	150.5
Main Grade	17.9	29.3	20.6	16.1	10.7	136.5
Basic Grade	18.5	33.1	21.6	16.0	12.7	160.9
Technical Grade I	15.1	33.3	25.0	16.0	12.7	150.9
Technical Grade II	13.6	32.7	24.3	24.4	7.3	150.3
Technical Grade III	18.0	30.5	25.0	29.0	4.6	159.6
Senior Draughtsman	23.5	30.1	22.6	16.1	12.7	157.5
Leading Draughtsman	23.9	28.3	25.2	24.4	7.3	165.6
Basic Draughtsman	24.7	27.8	27.1	29.0	4.6	172.8
Wages Index	12.0	25.5	18.9	21.5	12.4	128.2

Source: Adapted from Geoffrey K. Fry, 'Civil Service Salaries in the Post Priestley Era 1956-72', *Public Administration*, vol.52, Autumn 1974, pp.331-33.

Table 6 shows the rate of growth in various categories of civil servants' pay between 1956-72 (and for various sub-periods) compared to the general growth in wages over the same period.

If we consider the period 1956-72 as a whole, it appears that only 5 of the 27 occupational groups have experienced a lesser rate of increase than that of the general wage index: Executive Officer, Clerical Officer, Scientific Officer, Experimental Officer and Senior Scientific Assistant. It should be noted, however, that the number of staff involved in these grades was considerable, amounting to 40% of the non-industrial civil service at the time of the Fulton Commission report. Furthermore, at any point in time the number of occupations with cause for complaint in this regard may increase quite substantially. Certainly the periods of incomes policy seem to cause an increase in such numbers. For example, during the Prices and Incomes Board years of 1964-69, the Assistant Secretary, Principal, Executive Officer, Clerical Officer, Principal Scientific Officer, Junior Scientific Officer, Scientific Officer, and Experimental Officer grades all experienced a lesser rate of increase than that in the general wage index, while during the sub-period 1971-72 all of the Administrative, Executive and Clerical Grades, all Scientific grades and most of the Professional and Technical grades appeared to have cause for complaint. In short, the message from these figures is that while only a relatively small number of occupations suffered a below average rate of wage increase for the full period 1956-72, the number of occupations experiencing such a loss could increase considerably at any time, particularly during the years of operation of incomes policy.

The limitations of the above figures must, however, be noted in any attempt to fully assess the validity of the civil service unions' claim that they have suffered a disproportionate burden of wage restraint under periods of incomes policy. In general, any assessment of relative movements in pay is sensitive to the particular earnings series utilized and to the particular base date chosen for comparison purposes. But the more specific limitation of the figures in Table 6 for our purposes is that the civil service position is only compared with a general wage index. The fact of the matter is that such comparisons may mean little in terms of explaining the attitudes and behaviour of civil service unions if, although doing well in comparison with these average wage movements, they have lost out in relation to the *specific* occupational groups with which they have traditionally claimed comparability. It is particularly important to recall that these specific comparison groups are ment to be drawn not from a representative sample of outside employers but from a sub-sample of 'good' outside employers. This is important, because evidence (such as that in Table 6) that some grades in the civil service have lost out relative to average wage movements creates the presumption that an even larger number may have lost out in comparison with the wages of workers employed by the sub-sample of good, outside employers.

The implications of this point can be illustrated by taking another look at the figures in Table 6. On the basis of these figures it becomes difficult to account, at least *rationally*, for the obvious increase in various indices of industrial dissatisfaction in the civil service during the late 1960s and early 1970s. These were years which saw, for example, an increasing reluctance to appear before the civil service arbitration tribunal, the repeal of the no-strike clause in the constitution of the Civil Service Clerical Association in 1969 and the first official civil service strike in 1973. These various indices of dissatisfaction are all indicative of significant changes in the character of a number of civil service unions. According to the CSCA the essence of, and reasons for, this change were that

> The civil service is no longer unique in its conditions of service. The most distinctive features of civil service employment are now frequently matched and often improved upon in large, private firms. The future, if the most significant Fulton Committee recommendations are implemented, will produce a civil service almost indistinguishable in its attitude to staff and its conditions of employment from large private organizations. To the extent that these conditions change and the civil service becomes less of a 'protected industry' so will forms of trade union action change. If there is a desire, as there appears to be, to create a civil service on modern business lines, then it can be expected that civil service trade unionism will change to meet the new aggressive competitiveness inherent in such changes.[57]

The extent of concern about the changes in 'character', 'morale' and 'atmosphere' of the civil service in recent times is indicated by the creation of a Wider Issues Review Team in 1973.[58] If the figures in Table 6 are used to explain such changes in union attitudes and behaviour then one basically has to argue that 'the deterioration in civil service staff relations which took place in the late 1960s and early 1970s ... seemed to be imitative of the industrial militancy that characterized the general economic climate of the time.'[59] But *if* in fact what occurred was an earnings loss relative to the specific analogues with whom they have traditionally claimed comparability (i.e., the good, outside employers) then the situation in the civil service during this period does not have to rely on this 'imitative' type of argument as an explanation. There may instead have been a genuine basis for complaint within the civil service itself. There have, of course, been other hypotheses put forward to explain the 'increased militancy' in the civil service. It has, for example, been suggested that marked changes in the demographic and socio-economic structure and

TABLE 7

Average Weekly Earnings of Full Time Male Non-Manual Workers in National Government as a Percentage
of the Same in the Specified Industries, 1970-79

Industry/Year	1970	1971	1972	1973	1974	1975	1976	1977	1978	1979
Education Services	95.5	95.3	95.7	89.0	100.7	90.0	95.0	94.9	95.9	98.6
Local Government	110.6	104.0	103.5	94.8	106.5	97.3	104.4	104.1	103.6	99.2
Insurance	91.7*	89.4*	92.3*	88.1	97.5	92.6*	99.3*	97.7	90.4	88.0
Banking				82.7*	93.6*	91.5	96.3	91.6	86.4	85.3
Railways	118.2	109.9	114.7	99.1	112.6	99.4	109.7	107.4	104.6	104.1
Post Office	113.8	106.9	106.5	98.3	104.0	95.9	104.7	100.6	105.9	102.1

Source: New Earnings Survey, relevant years.

* The SIC order average.

composition of staff have been associated with significant changes in attitudes to authority and discipline. Other possible explanations include the increased geographical dispersion of the civil service workforce which has led to pressure on the highly centralized Whitley Committee-based structure.

It is not possible on the basis of available data to identify whether the non-industrial civil service has in fact gained or lost in relation to these specific, outside analogues. However, we did examine the industrial distribution of organizations included in the 1978 Pay Research Unit Study. The results indicate that fully 37% of the 458 surveys conducted were in the three industrial orders: insurance, banking, finance and business services (SIC XXIV), professional and scientific services (SIC XXV) and transport and communication (SIC XXII).[60] Accordingly, we selected the following industries from these orders: education services (SIC XXV); insurance, banking (SIC XXIV); and railways, postal services and telecommunications (SIC XXII). Local government was also chosen from SIC XXVII. We then calculated the average weekly earnings of male, non-manual employees in national government as a percentage of the average weekly earnings of male non-manuals in each of these industries for the years 1970-79. The results are set out in Table 7.

Table 7 reveals that male non-manual workers in national government had by the end of the decade lost ground relative to all the industries listed, except education services. The extent of loss to the insurance and banking sections was particularly marked in the latter half of the decade, which is in line with the general movement in favour of private sector earnings during these years.[61] A further point to note is the limitation of studies that have simply calculated changes in the ratio of average public to private sector earnings; the figures in Table 7 clearly indicate the heterogeneous nature of earnings movements in the different parts of the public sector. More generally, a simple comparison of the relative earnings position of national government employees in 1970 with that in 1979 is shown to be of limited value in view of the often very substantial year-to-year changes revealed in the table; witness, for example, the substantial relative gains for national government employees in 1973-74 and 1975-76, and the substantial relative losses in 1972-73 and 1974-75. The extent of these year-to-year changes is well illustrated in Table 8 which presents the annual percentage earnings increase for the industries listed in Table 7, as well as the all industries/services average and the average for the non-manufacturing sector.

The most striking individual feature of Table 8 is the highly variable nature of the size of increases in national government

47

TABLE 8

The Annual Increase in Average Weekly Earnings for Full Time Male Non-Manual Workers in the Specified Industries, 1970-71 — 1978-79

Industry/Year	1970-71	1971-72	1972-73	1973-74	1974-75	1975-76	197-77	1977-78	1978-79
National Government	7.5	18.9	6.0	27.8	18.8	29.8	4.9	10.2	9.2
Education Services	10.6	16.7	12.7	12.7	34.6	22.5	4.8	8.6	6.1
Local Government	15.2	17.9	14.8	12.8	30.2	20.3	5.4	10.2	14.3
Insurance	17.6*	13.5*	15.0	14.7	26.1*	19.9*	10.0	18.4	12.1
Banking			15.6*	14.3*	28.2	22.4	10.1	16.6	10.2
Railways	14.6	11.0	19.2	9.8	31.2	16.9	7.1	12.7	9.6
Post Office	13.1	15.9	11.4	19.6	31.8	18.7	9.1	4.6	13.2
All industries/services	12.9	13.5	13.1	15.0	27.5	19.1	8.7	13.0	11.9
Non-Manufacturing	13.4	15.0	13.3	15.7	27.9	19.8	8.5	12.1	11.1

Source: *New Earnings Survey*, relevant years

* The SIC order average.

compared to most of the other industries. National government increase was typically the highest for the industries listed in one year and then the lowest in the next year. The obvious question posed by this pattern is whether the relatively high increase in one year compensates for the relatively low increase of the previous year — in other words, is there sufficient catch-up to ensure that national government employees do not suffer a relative earnings loss over the period as a whole? The cumulative percentage increases for the years 1970-71 to 1978-79 were

National Government	133.1
Education Services	129.3
Local Government	141.1
Insurance	147.3
Banking	148.5
Railways	132.1
Post Office	137.4
All Industries/Services	134.7
Non-manufacturing	136.8

The figures suggest that the 'catch-up' for national government employees was not fully complete over the decade as a whole as all industries, except education services and railways, had a higher rate of cumulative increase. The losses in relation to the all industries/services and non-manufacturing averages were not particularly great, but were considerably more in the cases of insurance and banking which are arguably much closer to the specific outside analogues in the Pay Research Unit's surveys than are economy-wide or sectoral average figures. The figures in Tables 7 and 8 do help to put in some sort of context individual statistics, such as the 38.2% increase in the civil service wages/salaries bill in the financial year 1975-76, which are all too frequently cited in criticisms of the operation of the wage setting machinery for the non-industrial civil service.[62]

Has government acted as a best practice employer in relation to earnings? There is certainly some evidence, most notably concerning pensions and the disproportionate concentration on large-sized firms in the comparability surveys, to suggest that government may have provided terms and conditions of employment in excess of even those provided by the best of private sector employers. That this is widely believed is evidenced by the criticisms of many private sector employers and outside commentators, which in turn indicates the political pressures against the government assuming a model employer role where obvious, *direct* cost implications are involved. On the other hand, there is some evidence to suggest that close surveillance and tough treatment during periods of incomes policy is likely to have reduced any civil service wage differential (if it existed in the first place) quite considerably. Certainly the fact that some occupations in the civil service have suffered an earnings loss in relation to average earnings during such policy periods raises the strong likelihood that there has been an even greater loss, both in terms of the number of occupational groups concerned and the size of the actual loss, in comparison with the position of 'good' outside employers. The comparisons with male non-manual workers in certain selected industries over the decade of the seventies appear to support this suggestion. However, the ability to be more definite in this area is seriously constrained by the lack of detailed data for the specific outside analogues included in the Pay Research Unit's comparability surveys.

Chapter 4

Termination of Employment

That the civil service is at the centre of the non-market part of the British public sector has a number of important implications for employment relations, not least of which is limited pressure for termination of the employment contract through 'enforced' redundancies. The number of actual redundancies in the civil service over recent years is set out in Table 9.

TABLE 9

Persons Receiving Redundancy Compensation Payments under the 1965 and 1968 Acts, 1974-77 (Quarterly Figures)

Time Period	Total Number of Persons	Civil Service
1974 (1st Quarter)	40.573	558
1974 (2nd Quarter)	42,610	510
1974 (3rd Quarter)	41,225	483
1974 (4th Quarter)	57,753	485
1975 (1st Quarter)	70,657	413
1975 (2nd Quarter)	76,973	497
1975 (3rd Quarter)	100,840	345
1975 (4th Quarter)	91,745	303
1976 (1st Quarter)	95,391	440
1976 (2nd Quarter)	89,391	614
1976 (3rd Quarter)	68,518	640
1976 (4th Quarter)	60,428	367
1977 (1st Quarter)	72,204	374
1977 (2nd Quarter)	63,097	443
1977 (3rd Quarter)	66,684	550
1977 (4th Quarter)	65,249	638

Source: Relevant issues of the *Department of Employment Gazette.*

The figures indicate that not only have there been few redundancies in the civil service, but those that do occur are largely independent of the movement in the total number of redundancies in the economy —

they are more the outcome of civil service-specific factors than the result of adverse system-wide economic pressures. The very size of the civil service is also important in accounting for the relatively small number of declared redundancies — there is considerable scope for job losses to be met by natural wastage and internal mobility rather than through redundancy. The Priestley Commission certainly contended that the 'good' employer is one who 'seeks ... to provide stability and continuity of employment', but the relative insulation of the civil service from adverse product market forces means that it is hardly 'fair' to private sector employers to take the figures in Table 9 as evidence that the government is a best practice employer.

Redundancies and procedural justice

Much more relevant in this regard is the existence of an explicit, detailed *jointly agreed procedure* for handling redundancies in the civil service. Indeed, the very absence of redundancies as a sizeable union-management problem makes the existence of such procedural arrangements so impressive. This is because theories of management or organizational behaviour, such as contingency theory, tend to suggest that structure or procedures tend to come about only in response to the pressure of 'sizeable problems'.

The *current* arrangements for dealing with redundancy can be placed in a broader context of 'premature retirement', a detailed agreement which was negotiated in 1971-72. Subsequently a specific agreement on redundancy arrangements was negotiated in 1975 (the details of which are set out in Appendix I). The current procedures for dealing with redundancy represent an updating and revision of arrangements that have existed for a number of years. A survey of over 350 firms conducted by the Department of Employment in 1963 found that the few explicit, detailed policies for dealing with redundancies were typically far less comprehensive than arrangements in the civil service (and the public sector more generally) with regard to the extent of consultation with employee representatives, provision of extra notice or advance warning, provision of severance payments, and reference to pension rights.[1] This imbalance of treatment has been summarized in the following terms:

> There is ... something of a dual standard for public — and private — sector employers in the United Kingdom. In coal-mining, on the railways and, more recently, in British Steel, redundancy procedures have been humane and generous. More effort has gone into finding the least troublesome methods of slimming down these industries' payrolls than in common among private sector organizations. Apart from paying quite large sums of money to employees

dismissed on grounds of redundancy, public-sector enterprises have bent over backwards to moderate the social and psychological disagreeableness of collective dismissals. Where the public sector has scored time and time again is in terms of deliberation and long-term preparation. From this have sprung elements of positive redevelopment which are strikingly unusual in arrangements made by private firms in Britain.[2]

The civil service is not explicitly mentioned in the above quote, but it has obviously been, in keeping with the rest of the public sector, a best practice employer in terms of its detailed, jointly agreed procedural arrangements for dealing with redundancies. The existence of such arrangements certainly accords well with the Priestley Committee's view that the good employer consults with representatives of his employees upon all changes affecting conditions of work.

The hope that civil service practice, and that of the public sector more generally, would spread to the private sector is evidenced by a Department of Employment document issued in 1968 setting out good practice guidelines for handling redundancies 'based on the practice of progressive managements'.[3] This document emphasised the importance of forward planning and advance arrangements in handling redundancies, discussed individual issues such as the phasing of redundancies, selection for redundancies, the provision of notice and assistance in finding other employment, and particularly stressed the need for full and detailed consultation with employee representatives at all stages. This exercise (the document has been updated and re-issued) has been the only attempt made to transfer civil service and public sector practice, to the private sector. The effect in the private sector of this 'code of practice' has been seen to be relatively slight since 'like all pieces of exhortation, the ideas set out in *Dealing with Redundancies* have nothing more than moral authority, and managers of enterprises are at liberty to ignore any or all of them. Employers are offered no rewards or punishments if they fail to introduce domestic procedures for handling redundancies.'[4] Although there is no precise way of assessing the influence of these good practice guidelines, it is apparent that few establishments had detailed, jointly agreed arrangements for handling redundancies in the late sixties and early seventies. For example, a survey carried out in 1969 for the Department of Employment reported that only 15% of the sampled establishments had an agreement or understanding with trade unions about redundancy.[5]

There were additional guidance documents issued in the early 1970s urging private sector employers to consult more fully with employee representatives over the means of declaring redundancies. For example, the Code of Practice under the Industrial Relations Act 1971 urged such consultation, while the Commission on Industrial Relations saw the measures for dealing with redundancies as matters in which unions had a legitimate interest in the disclosure of information.[6] However, it eventually proved necessary, under the pressure of involvement in the European Economic Community, to provide for joint consultation over procedures for handling redundancies on a *statutory* basis (through the stipulated provisions of Part IV of the Employment Protection Act 1975). The very fact that such legislation was considered necessary could be interpreted as tacit evidence that the good practice guidelines had not been thought sufficiently effective in encouraging private sector employers to voluntarily establish such procedural arrangements. This suggestion should, however, be seen in the context of a survey undertaken for the Department of Employment in 1977 which found that these statutory provisions for consultation over redundancy had relatively little impact on employers since such procedural arrangements were already in existence.[7] The voluntary establishment of such arrangements may, however, have owed more to union pressure in the adverse economic circumstances of the early seventies than to the influence of good practice guidelines, although the latter may have been of some importance in shaping the content of these actual arrangements.

Discipline and dismissals more generally

Termination of the employment contract through redundancy, together with procedures for handling the resulting redundancies, can be placed in the broader context of arrangements for premature retirement on (i) the grounds of limited efficiency; (ii) structural grounds; (iii) on grounds of inefficiency and (iv) on medical grounds. Following a number of recommendations in the report of the Fulton Committee an agreement on premature retirement was reached with the National Staff Side in 1971. (The current code of practice derived from this agreement is reproduced as Appendix 2.) A key aspect of this agreement was the decision to establish an independent board to which any non-industrial civil servant under notice of dismissal or premature retirement may appeal. The Board applies two criteria in assessing the fairness of the intended action: (i) has the management acted fairly and in accordance with the procedures agreed between management and staff representatives? and (ii) is premature retirement or dismissal the right or most appropriate action to take? The Board heard 648 appeals between 1972-78.[8] A civil servant under notice of premature retirement or dismissal may also appeal to an industrial tribunal. Although we have no specific figures, there appear to have been few such unfair dismissal applications made; for example, only 1.7% of the total number of unfair dismissal applications during

1972-75 occurred in 'public administration' (local government as well as central government), a figure well below the proportion of the workforce employed in this sector.[9] This is obviously consistent with the point made in the introductory section that, although the government has insisted on maintaining its right to dismissal at will, the detailed, jointly-agreed procedures of the civil service have been a powerful force against arbitrary dismissal.

The code of practice on dismissal procedures was issued in 1976 but, as with the procedures for handling redundancies, detailed arrangements along these lines have existed in the civil service for some little time.[10] This raises the question of whether these civil service practices have had any influence on private sector employers. A recent study of disciplinary procedures and practices based on a survey of 267 private sector companies argued that 'no report on company disciplinary practice would be complete without some reference to the influence of Government and quasi-governmental bodies on disciplinary issues.'[11] This report specifically found that 50% of the companies surveyed had made changes to their disciplinary procedures in the last two years for their manual and/or non-manual employees, a fact which they largely attributed (rather than clearly established) to the favourable influence of government or quasi-government issued codes of practice. The conclusion of this study is interesting as it constitutes a counter-weight to the frequently expressed view that the influence of civil service good employer practice as transmitted through codes of practice is likely to be limited in encouraging private sector employers to follow suit. Although the results clearly do not refute this view, they do suggest the value of research designed to assess the impact and influence of these codes of practice.

The evidence reviewed in this section indicates that the government has sought to act as a best practice employer and provide a lead for other employers in the treatment of issues surrounding the termination of the employment contract. What is less certain is the extent to which this lead has been followed. The necessity for legislation on procedures for handling redundancies lends support to the view that the government lead has not been widely emulated on a voluntary basis. On the other hand, at least one study has suggested (at least in the area of disciplinary procedures) that this example of the government via codes of practice has not been a trivial influence on private sector employers. Further studies should be undertaken to allow us to provide a more comprehensive account of the extent of government influence in this particular area.

Chapter 5

Conclusions

Has government, at least in our selected subject areas in the civil service, sought both in principle and in practice to act as a best practice employer? Where it has sought to act in this way, has this example had any obvious, positive impact in raising standards in the private sector?

A summary of findings

Although the inevitable data deficiencies have hindered our attempt to fully answer these questions, the picture that emerges can be summarized as follows:

Government has sought to act as a best practice employer by voluntarily taking on the obligation to employ a quota of registered disabled employees, but its actual compliance rate in this regard has tended to be below the average for the private sector; the latter itself being a far from impressive performance. In the employment of racial minority workers in the civil service the government can claim to be a best practice employer in having an explicit equal opportunity policy and, perhaps more importantly, in having attempted at least a preliminary monitoring of the policy's effects; the latter is certainly something that few private sector employers can claim. However, the preliminary monitoring of the practical effects of this policy suggests that workers suffering the accumulated effects of past discrimination may face considerable difficulties in meeting civil service standards of recruitment and promotion.

In keeping with the stated commitments to encourage collective bargaining, government has clearly acted as a best practice employer in encouraging union organization and collective bargaining arrangements in the civil service. This encouragement can be seen as an attempt to aid the efficient, internal operation of the civil service, and to set an example for private sector employers. An examination of the operation and impact of the Fair Wages Resolution, however, seems to suggest that its example in this regard has had little substantive impact on private sector practice.

The provisions of the Priestley Commission certainly committed the government to act as a good employer in wage terms in the civil service. However, it has been claimed that certain biases in the operation of the Priestley Committee recommendations have caused civil service pay to be in advance of that provided by good, outside employers. Although some individual pieces of evidence are consistent with this line of argument, there is also some apparent support for claims that government has in practice dishonoured its good employer obligation by seeking to apply the terms of incomes policies most rigorously in the civil service. However, the lack of detailed and comprehensive data on the *full range* of terms and conditions of civil service employees, together with that for the specific analogues included in the comparability surveys, limits the ability of outside researchers to reconcile these apparently conflicting lines of argument. The real value of our examination of the pay issue in relation to the good and model employer notions is that it highlights the considerable range of pressures and influences on government in its employer role. In this sense these notions, which are considerably broader than those typically adopted by researchers looking at pay movements in the civil service, appear to have considerable analytical value.

In matters concerning the termination of the employment contract government has undoubtedly acted as a best practice employer in the civil service in having detailed, jointly-agreed arrangements to ensure 'procedural justice' for the employees concerned. Again, however, the extent to which this example has influenced private sector practice remains questionable.

Difficulties of influencing the private sector

Why is there so little *obvious* evidence that the best practice example of government as an employer has favourably influenced private sector practice? Although this was not the major reason for government acting in this manner, it appears to have been anticipated as an important secondary effect and as such is worthy of some examination. The 'academic' literature is full of numerous, but often rather glib, recommendations for government to introduce new innovations in working conditions and practices.[1] There are two basic, but quite different answers to the above question. The first is that the absence of profit and loss considerations allows government the luxury of being a best practice employer; therefore, civil service experience of innovation in terms and conditions of employment will be of little guidance to the private sector. The contention here is that a basic paradox exists in the best practice employer notion which means, as was suggested in relation to the equal pay issue, that 'We have to reckon with the possibility that the lead which is being demanded in some quarters from Government ... might prove to be a false lead, a real equality within the public services being taken as a precedent for establishing, with very different results, a false equality elsewhere.'[2] In short, the argument is that the very factors which allow government to adopt best employer practices mean that civil service experience will not be a representative guide to the full implications of change in the private sector.

The above argument does not seem entirely convincing. It views government as an employer much less constrained than the typical private sector employer but sees the relevant constraints only in rather narrow profit and loss terms. In fact, the government operates under a greater degree of accountability and answerability than the average private sector employer because of the range of pressures and influences on it. This is especially illustrated by our earlier discussions of the wage issue in relation to the model and good employer notions. The nature of these diverse influences and pressures on government is also evidenced during public sector strikes; third party pressures and public opinion make strikes in the public sector a political, rather than strictly economic, weapon.[3] Accordingly, the decision to act as a best practice employer is a far from costless one for government, as is implicitly assumed by the above argument. This is not to deny, however, that general and specific economic circumstances have been important in constraining private sector employers to follow the government's lead. As Bienfeld noted in relation to the hours of work issue,

> The failure of extensive reductions in hours sponsored by the government to precipitate wide-spread reductions makes the point: neither the Textile Acts, nor the Coal Mines Acts, nor the adoption of the eight hour day in many government establishments in 1894, led to any subsequent general reductions, even though such expressions of government attitudes might be thought to auger well for attempts at reduction elsewhere. In fact these changes did not lead to general reductions because they came at times when in many of the large unions the demand for reduced hours was not strong, or when their bargaining position was weak. ... All this suggests that the cause of the periods of reduction must be sought in the general economic circumstances which influenced the preferences of employers and employees alike.[4]

A second and rather more optimistic answer, at least in terms of longer-run possibilities for favourable change, to the question of why the government's best practice example has not been more widely emulated in the private sector is that government has failed to establish a sufficiently powerful, institutionalized mechanism for affecting the transfer of practice across to the private sector. The government has frequently tended to rely, as in the case of procedures for handling redundancies, on the weak techniques of publicity and exhortation. In other cases an explicit, institutional link with the private sector has been established via government contractors, the potential importance of which can be gauged from the fact that an estimate of the late 1960s suggested that government procurement absorbed approximately 5% of the total output of the manufacturing and construction sector.[5] The imposition of special obligations on these contractors, together with a serious administrative commitment (in terms of both manpower resources and the use and severity of sanctions) to the monitoring of compliance, could perhaps go a considerable way to ensuring the transfer of best employer practices to the private sector. The experience with the racial equality clause and the Fair Wages Resolution is, however, a salutary reminder of the need for a serious administrative backup to the simple imposition of obligations if this attempt to aid the transfer process is to be anything more than a token gesture.

The approach outlined above will not, however, be without its difficulties. The first and most obvious point is that there will inevitably be political objections from the private sector if a large-scale attempt is made to impose and monitor an extensive set of best practice employer obligations on government contractors. The sort of reaction that can be expected will not be too dissimilar from that which occurred in response to the previous Labour Government's attempt to ensure that government contractors strictly conformed to incomes policy guidelines.[6] The other possible difficulty with this recommendation is that government contractors may be an unrepresentative sub-set of private sector employers; they may, for example, be disproportionately numbered among large-sized firms who would be among the best practice private sector employers anyway. If this is, in fact, the case then the imposition of best practice obligations will constitute little hardship and should thus provoke little adverse political reaction. But one may return to the contention that the government's particular experience with any employment innovation may constitute little real guide to effects that would typically be experienced in the private sector. However, even if detailed research on the characteristics of government contractors found them to be an atypical group of private sector employers at any point in time it would be possible, for example, to deliberately orient government contracts to smaller establishments, a course of action alleged to be favoured by the present Government.

Good employer practice — an iron law?

This discussion about the means for effectively transferring best employer practices from the civil service to the private sector assumes that government will continue to act in such a manner in its treatment of civil service employees. Best employer practice in the civil service is not an iron law, completely insulated from any significant changes in government policy. Indeed we have already discussed at some length the claim that this good practice obligation has already been dishonoured as government has downgraded its responsibilities to its own employees in relation to those to the public at large during periods of incomes policies. A more specific example was the passage of the Trade Disputes and Trade Unions Act of 1927, immediately following the General Strike, which, among other things, forbade public authorities from demanding union membership of employees and stipulated criminal liabilities for strikes calculated to 'coerce' the government; this Act was hardly invoked in practice and was repealed in 1946. Potentially more significant are the present Conservative Government's policies of cash limits and public expenditure cuts which raise the very real possibility of a significant step back from best employer practice, at least in certain respects. The Government's policy of public expenditure cuts is viewed as a strategy for improving the macro or aggregate performance of the economy; in this regard the 'too few producers' line of argument associated with the work of Eltis and Bacon is obviously of considerable influence, as are the monetarist doctrines of economists such as Milton Friedman.[7] There is also an important industrial relations aim to the present Government's policy of public expenditure cuts, which stems from the belief that unions in the public service are in an especially powerful bargaining position and that this power needs to be curbed.

This 'excess union power in the public sector' belief should be seen in the context of the 'general state' of public sector industrial relations during the 1970s. These were years that witnessed, for example, the first nationwide strikes by local authority, fire brigade and some post office and civil service employees. Furthermore, a number of these strikes were directed more again government policy than against the immediate employing authorities — they were basically protests against the restrictions of incomes policy.

The importance of industrial relations considerations in Conservative Party thinking is indicated by a report prepared by a party committee under Lord Carrington.[8] This report, which was prompted by the confrontations between the Heath Government and the miners in 1972 and 1974, expressed considerable doubts about any government's ability to deal with powerful unions in the public sector. More recently, the *Sunday Times* leaked some confidential Cabinet Office papers which set out a number of Government priority objectives for the medium and longer term, among which were proposals to 'deprivilege' the civil service and curb the power of civil service unions.[9]

The basis of the belief in the strong power of unions in the civil service, and in the public sector more generally, can be expressed as follows:

> Firstly, whereas there are many substitutes for the commodities supplied by most private firms, typically there are no adequate substitutes for the commodities supplied by the government, for the most part because such substitutes are banned by statute. In consequence, the costs of a strike to the general public tend to be higher in the public than in the private sector. Secondly, whereas strikes in the private sector (even when subsidised by the State) must be tempered by the need to protect the viability of the firms involved, no such consideration is required with strikes in the public sector. In consequence, strike behaviour in the public sector tends to be more prolonged and not infrequently to involve malicious damage to the assets at risk. For whereas the revenues of private firms dry up over the duration of a strike, taxes are still levied by the government to pay for non-existent commodities and to subsidize the strike itself when public provisions are suspended. Both features offer advantages to public sector unions in wage negotiations. These advantages tend to be compounded by the nature of employer bargaining within the public sector. For the government negotiator, knowing that wage concessions can be passed on in taxes which citizens cannot refuse to pay, and recognizing the public pressure to settle strikes in statute-enforced monopolistic markets, often has more to fear in immediate voter discontent from a strike than from the tax increase required to settle it. For the taxes will not be required immediately and will be spread over the public at large whereas the specific interests damaged by the strike have every incentive to lobby vociferously for a settlement. Furthermore, the politicians who are bargaining recognize that elections may be won by gaining the support of well organized groups prepared to channel money and effort into the next campaign. By acquiescing in excessive wage demands, politicians may obtain valuable election support, especially in countries like Britain where a sizeable electoral group is employed in the public sector.[10]

In summary, the central argument underlying the public sector union power thesis is that these unions are in the especially favourable position of being relatively insulated from competitive market forces since their employer is a monopolist; this means that high wage gains will not have any adverse employment consequences for their members. The result is that collective bargaining in the public sector is simply a wages bargain with the union leadership not having to moderate their wage demands for fear of displacing some of their members from employment; in the private sector collective bargaining is much more likely to approximate a wages-employment bargain. Although this argument is open to both theoretical and empirical criticism[11] one can characterize the present Government's strategy of cash limits-expenditure cuts as an attempt to tighten the relationship between wages and employment in the public sector and thus reduce the extent of union power.

In the matter of expenditure cuts, the Government announced in December 1979 a decision to make savings in civil service staff costs of £212 million, which would be equivalent to 39,000 posts. A Civil Service Department memorandum suggested that the approximate distribution between the non-industrial and industrial civil service would be 28,000 and 11,000 respectively. The initial provisional estimates of the value of gross savings over the next four years, and the approximate reductions in posts, were:

Year	Gross Savings (cumulative)	Reduction in Posts (cumulative)
1980-1	£65m	12,000
1981-2	£135m	24,000
1982-3	£200m	37,000
1983-4	£212m	39,000

This reduction was only half the minimum option (10%) that each minister had been asked to explore, a fact which led a *Sunday Times* article to suggest that 'What started out as an exercise in rolling back the frontiers of government has so far failed to do more than dent the boundary line in a few places. On present plans there will still be more white collar civil servants in three years time than there were when the Conservatives were last in office.'[12] However, the press reported in late April 1980 that proposals were being mooted to make a further reduction in the civil service; the Prime Minister's aim was reported to be a reduction in the number of civil servants to 600,000 in time for the next election.[13] This report drew an angry response from Bill Kendall, general secretary of the Council of Civil Service Unions (formerly the staff side of the National Whitley Council), who stated that civil service unions bitterly resented hearing about the proposals for a new round of cuts in the press rather than through established channels of consultation. This claim should be seen in the context of the Priestley Commission's statement that an important component of good employer practice was the provision of adequate procedures for consultation over changes affecting the employment of civil servants. In response to this particular union criticism the head of the home civil service, Sir Ian Bancroft, gave an assurance that proper consultation procedures would be respected 'whatever may follow'.

The question of whether the proposed civil service employment cuts, in conjunction with the system of cash limits, will successfully 'moderate' the size of civil service pay settlements has been thrown into some doubt by the settlement announced in April 1980. The cash limit for civil service spending on pay was reported in early April to allow for an increase of 14% which, together with the 2.5% manpower cut, suggested a final settlement figure of around 16.8%. In fact, the average pay increase for all grades in a full year was 18.75%, a figure that the *Sunday Times* argued made meaningless the Government's contention that pay and output must be strictly linked.[14] A further element of uncertainty about the likely effectiveness of the Government's policy strategy in moderating the size of civil service wage settlements, and those in the public sector more generally, was added by the Chancellor of the Exchequer's statement (subsequently retracted) later that month that the Government had actually budgeted for a 25% rise in the wages of civil servants and its other employees this year.[15]

The present Government is also strongly in favour of ending the index-linking of a variety of social benefits. As part of this general approach, consideration has been given to possible changes in the 'controversial' system of index-linked pensions for civil servants. This is a matter currently under review, although civil service unions have warned that any attempt to make substantial changes to existing arrangements will result in industrial action.[16] However, it seems likely that some changes in these arrangements will be made, given the Government's apparent intention to 'deprivilege' the civil service and reduce union power. If this does occur then it would illustrate our earlier proposition that best employer practice in the civil service is certainly not completely insulated from sharp changes in government policy-making priorities. It will be unfortunate if this proposition is most dramatically illustrated by a sharp confrontation between the civil service unions and the government, a far from remote possibility.

APPENDIX 1

MODEL REDUNDANCY AGREEMENT

GENERAL

1. These arrangements are intended to form the basis of any redundancy agreement or procedures operated by departments and covering their non-industrial staff. They also complement those already agreed in the National Whitley Council's 'Agreement on Arrangements and Compensation for Premature Retirement', the compensation provisions of which will apply. It is recognized that different situations may require different methods, and that the size of the department concerned will be a relevant factor but the arrangements below should be followed wherever appropriate by departments in negotiating new departmental agreements and operating redundancy schemes in full consultation with the staff interests concerned. It is essential that consultation with staff interests should be commenced at the earliest possible stage and then be a continuing feature, for the resolution by agreement of a situation of staff surplus or redundancy. This area is recognized as being essentially a matter for the closest co-operation between Official and Staff Sides. The arrangements outlined in paragraph 2 below (which are not intended to denote any order or priority) should be fully explored before any redundancy situation is declared.

ACTION REQUIRED BEFORE REDUNDANCY IS DECLARED

2. When it is clear that there is likely to be a surplus of staff in any given area of work, a redundancy situation should not be declared until the following have been considered in full consultation with the appropriate staff interests:

(a) a review of the present and future work pattern of the department to ensure that a surplus of staff is unavoidable;

(b) transfer of staff within the department to other areas of work where there are suitable vacancies;

(c) transfers of staff to other civil service departments (or to fringe bodies) where work is available;

(d) if no vacancies, capable of being filled by surplus mobile staff, exist in the appropriate or similar grades in any other departments, suitable staff in similar grades from outside the redundancy fields who would be prepared to volunteer for retirement would be considered for premature retirement in place of those who would otherwise be redundant. This would arise firstly within the department itself but if insufficient volunteers were found there, volunteers from other departments should be sought. With the consent of the importing department concerned, the staff who would otherwise be redundant in the exporting department would fill the vacancies created by such volunteers. The latter would then be retired on public interest terms even though in such circumstances a state of redundancy had not then been established.

(e) staff remaining in their existing grade for a limited period but being overborne against a lower grade post in a situation where the availability of a post in the existing grade is foreseen.

(f) recruitment and/or promotion reduced or suspended within the department and the remainder of the civil service where similar grades, disciplines or blocks of work exist unless it is agreed that this does not offer an effective way of reducing or resolving the redundancy situation.

(g) a review of the age of retirement practice within the department concerned in order to deal with the staff surplus problem. This would not be inconsistent with the provisions of paragraph 4 below.

65

(h) the re-training of staff as follows:

(i) re-training for other jobs within the civil service and fringe bodies within the locality of staff surplus (mainly for non-mobile staff, mobile staff being covered by ii. below)

(ii) re-training for other jobs within the civil service or fringe bodies either within an existing specialization or one close to that already held.

(j) subject to specific Staff Side agreement in the unit of redundancy concerned, consideration should be given to the temporary blocking of posts vacant in junior grades in the same class or occupational group (or in another group by agreement with the recognized staff association representing the junior grades) by senior staff.

3. When after all the measures set out in paragraph 2 have been explored a redundancy is declared, units of redundancy should operate as follows:

(a) mobile staff — the unit of redundancy would cover all members of the grade concerned in the department affected. In some instances, where the grade itself is divided into different specialisms, the unit of redundancy might be less in the light of the demands of a particular situation. In the case of Under Secretary level redundancy, the unit would be service-wide;

(b) non-mobile staff — the unit of redundancy would cover all the members of the grade concerned in the department affected, in the area within daily travelling distance of the particular establishment giving rise to the redundancy. Opportunity should be made, however, for volunteers to transfer to vacancies in other departments in the same area or to other areas if they so desire.

ORDER OF DISCHARGE

4. In the event of discharge of surplus staff being unavoidable, the following order of discharge will apply:

(i) casual staff, and staff employed by contractors or private employment agencies who are working for, or within the department;

(ii) unestablished staff over age 65, oldest first;

(iii) established staff over age 65, oldest first;

(iv) staff (both established and unestablished) who are prepared to volunteer for premature retirement (i.e. under paragraph 22 of the 'Agreement on Arrangements and Compensation for Premature Retirement') within the redundancy field;

(v) staff aged between 60 and 65 with 40 years or more reckonable service for superannuation purposes, oldest first;

(vi) unestablished staff and those on period appointments on a 'last in, first out' basis;

(vii) staff aged between 60 and 65 with less than 40 years reckonable service for superannuation purposes, those with most pension entitlement first;

(viii) all other staff on a 'last in, first out' basis subject to the right of management to retain staff on grounds of individual ability or specialist knowledge acquired as a result of special training at the cost of the department.

Note: Individual posts — it is, of course, not necessarily the office holder who falls to be retired if he is one of the number of staff similarly qualified to fill the post which is being abolished.

5. In deciding on a relative position amongst staff over the minimum retirement age, regard should be given to the need to maximize the pension entitlement of individuals. With regard to categories (vi) and (viii) the 'last in, first out' criterion should apply

unless specific agreement to the contrary is reached with the appropriate Staff Side. Where departments wish to depart from this rule they should always first offer premature retirement terms to those who are prepared to volunteer on this basis. Reckonable service for the 'last in, first out' criterion would cover all who are prepared to volunteer on this basis. Reckonable service for the 'last in, first out' criterion would cover all time spent in the non-industrial civil service. Except where there is no normal expectation of career progression, industrial service would also count for this purpose. Only unbroken service, i.e. service which is both continuous and immediately precedes redundancy, would be reckonable. In applying the above criteria, regard should be had to the protection of the existing quota (3%) of registered disabled staff in the civil service and to persons who had transferred into the service with their work in circumstances where the service took over functions formerly carried out by other parts of the public service.

ASSISTANCE TO STAFF DECLARED REDUNDANT

6. *Spreading the Redundancy Programme.* The fullest notice should be given of all likely and actual redundancy programmes, and the existence of residual work in the winding-up period should be used to spread the programme over as long a period as possible compatible with the efficient management of the redundancy unit. This should maximize the extent to which normal wastage can be used to solve redundancy problems.

7. *Pay and Pension Treatment and Downgrading.* Redundant officers may request voluntary downgrading to fill a vacant post, or be offered down-grading to a vacant post as an alternative to redundancy compensation. Downgrading to a vacant post in these circumstances will, however, be on a mark-time basis. The pay treatment will be that generally available on reversion or downgrading. The person downgraded will, however, be given the choice at the point of final retirement of being pensioned for his whole service on the best year in his last 3 years' salary; or for treating separately his earlier service before downgrading, thus drawing separate pensions for the two periods of service; the latter arrangement will, in some cases, be advantageous to the employee.

8. *Re-training.* Where vacancies exist in the service or in fringe bodies for which redundant staff would be suitable subject only to a limited amount of re-training, appropriate training will be given provided the staff are in other ways suitable. Re-training of a more general nature would more appropriately be undertaken on the personal initiative of those concerned, but CSD would offer advice and guidance wherever possible (see paragraph 2.h.above).

9. *Resettlement.* When redundancies occur, departments should appoint a resettlement officer to advise and assist staff who are redundant in finding alternative posts within or outside the civil service, and with re-training or other problems arising from the redundancy. If specialist staff are involved an officer with knowledge of their problems should be available to assist with resettlement. The Professional and Executive Register of the Department of Employment should also be consulted.

10. *Period of Notice.* During the period of notice (which would be at least that in the 'Agreement on Arrangements and Compensation for Premature Retirement') time off on full pay should be allowed to attend interviews for other posts. The period of notice will be extended beyond that shown in the above agreement whenever possible, particularly when long-service staff are involved in the redundancy.

CODE OF PRACTICE ON PREMATURE RETIREMENT

INTRODUCTION

10510. This section of the Code gives details of the circumstances in which an officer may be retired before he has reached his minimum retirement age, as defined in the Code section, Superannuation, paragraphs 8572 to 8574. All the provisions in this section are applicable to industrial as well as non-industrial staff except those relating to retirement on grounds of inefficiency; the appropriate procedures for industrial staff in this respect are set out in CSDIM(73)20 and CSDIM(75)10.

10511. An officer may be prematurely retired:
a. on grounds of limited efficiency; (retirement on these grounds is regarded as
b. on structural grounds; retirement in the public interest)
c. on grounds of inefficiency; and
d. on medical grounds (it should be noted that retirement on medical grounds can be effected after as well as before minimum retirement age).
An officer may also be prematurely retired on redundancy grounds, but the appropriate provisions are set out in the Code section, Redundancy.

10512. The compensation terms applicable to retirement on grounds of limited efficiency, structural grounds and grounds of inefficiency are in the Code section, Superannuation (Compulsory Premature Retirement). The superannuation provisions applicable to retirement for medical reasons are in the Code section, Superannuation (Ill Health Retirement).

10513-10522. Unallocated.

RETIREMENT IN THE PUBLIC INTEREST

10523-10527 unallocated.

Period of Notice

10528. An officer will be given as much informal notice as practicable, and, if his department contemplates retirement on grounds of limited efficiency, he will be given specific prior warnings that an improvement in his performance is necessary. All established staff will always be given 6 months formal notice. Unestablished staff with 2 years service but less than 5 years will be given not less than 3 months formal notice. Unestablished staff with less than 2 years service will be given at least the notice required by the contracts of employment legislation, and departments will give the maximum amount of notice possible. If the department is unable to provide work for the whole of the minimum period of notice, the officer will be paid for the unexpired portion; but this will not be done if he leaves voluntarily with the agreement of his department before the end of his period of notice.

10529-10533 unallocated.

Limited efficiency

10534. A civil servant in the mobile category whose performance no longer adequately measures up to the requirements of his post, or who fails to carry out his full duties satisfactorily, may be retired on grounds of limited efficiency. If the prior warnings referred to in paragraph 10528 fail to produce an acceptable improvement in the officer's performance a retirement board will be set up to consider his case and recommend what action should be taken.

10535. The officer will be told of the retirement board's recommendation and of his rights of appeal. If the retirement board recommends that he should be retired he will be given at least 6 months formal notice of his retirement. If he contests retirement, he has the right to appeal to the Civil Service Appeal Board, in accordance with the procedures set out in the Code section of that name. He will be given a copy of the memorandum his personnel division will have prepared setting out the reasons for his retirement. The supporting evidence submitted to the Appeal Board will need to include his recent annual reports, together with any other relevant documents, e.g. appraisal reports, and the Appeal Board will have power, on application by the officer, to require the department to give him access to relevant papers, including annual reports which it considers to be necessary for him to see for the adequate presentation of his case.

Structural grounds

10536. Staff in mobile grades may be prematurely retired on structural grounds, for example when there is a very bad age distribution in a particular group of staff leading to serious promotion blockage and consequent difficulty in the management of that part of the Service. No-one below Senior Principal level can be compelled to retire on these grounds; but departments may use premature retirement to deal with structural problems at lower levels provided that those retired are prepared to go willingly.

10537-10545 unallocated.

INEFFICIENCY

10546. The provisions of paragraphs 10547 to 10566 apply to non-industrial staff only. For the procedures applicable to industrial staff see CSDIM(73)20 and CSDIM(75)10.

10547. An officer may be prematurely retired on grounds of inefficiency if he has been judged no longer able to discharge his duties efficiently because:

a. his work performance has deteriorated to an unacceptable standard; or

b. his frequent absences from work adversely affect the efficient running of his office.

In order to ensure that the decision to retire an officer in either of these circumstances is taken after full investigation, with proper safeguards for the individual concerned, the procedures set out in paragraphs 10553 to 10566 are followed.

10548-10552 unallocated.

Officers whose performance has deteriorated

10553. The officer will always be given prior informal warning that his performance is falling below the acceptable standard. Every effort will be made to give him time, opportunity and assistance to improve, and to discover the cause of any sudden deterioration. If it is thought that the drop in performance, whether gradual or sudden, is likely to be due to health reasons or if the officer maintains that this is so, he will be advised to consult his doctor. He will be warned that unless an improvement in his performance can be effected with his doctor's help, the department may have to initiate formal procedure which could lead to his being prematurely retired either on grounds of inefficiency or on medical grounds.

10554. If, after the informal warning procedure outlined above has been carried out, there has been insufficient improvement, formal procedure for compulsory premature retirement on grounds of inefficiency will be initiated by an adverse report by the operational manage; this may be submitted at any time and need not await the normal reporting date. The officer will then be formally warned in writing that his performance is unacceptable and told the reasons.

10555. After the formal written warning the officer will be put on trial for a period of at least 6 months, whenever possible in a different suitable post under another manager. If it seems likely, and the officer agrees or suggests himself, that the poor performance may be attributable to medical causes, he will be told at this stage that the case is being put to the Civil Service Medical Adviser, but that if the Medical Adviser does not recommend, or if the officer contests, retirement on medical grounds the procedure for retirement on grounds of inefficiency will be initiated if his performance does not improve.

10556. At the end of the 6 months trial period a further report will be called for. If this is also adverse the question of the officer's retirement will be considered by a retirement board. The officer can, if he wishes, appear before the board with a friend, who may be a staff representative. If the board then recommends retirement, its findings will be confirmed and the officer told. An officer under notice of retirement on grounds of inefficiency has a right to appeal to the Civil Service Appeal Board in accordance with the prescribed procedures.

10557-10561 unallocated.

Officers whose attendance is regarded as unsatisfactory

10562. If an officer who is efficient while at work fails to give satisfactory service because of frequent or continuous absences (arising mainly from minor non-recurrent ailments), measures may be taken to terminate his appointment.

10563. If it is decided to initiate premature retirement proceedings, the officer will be warned informally that his attendance is unsatisfactory and efforts will be made to determine the reason for his poor attendance. If insufficient improvement results, formal procedure will be initiated for compulsory premature retirement on grounds of inefficiency arising from unsatisfactory attendance, i.e., a formal written warning will be given and the officer will afterwards be put on a trial period of at least 6 months, whenever possible in a different suitable post under another manager.

10564. If at this stage the department thinks, or the officer himself suggests, that the unsatisfactory attendance results from a medical condition which would make retirement on medical grounds appropriate, he will be told that his case is to be put to the Civil Service Medical Adviser. He will also be informed of his rights, which include the adoption of one of the following courses if, after consulting his doctor, he considers that his circumstances justify it:

(a) to have his case referred to the Medical Adviser on the grounds that his condition will improve; or

(b) to apply for medical retirement and, if his application is unsuccessful, to appeal to a medical board in accordance with paragraphs 10585 to 10598.

10565. If by the end of the 6 month trial period there has been no adequate improvement, the retirement board procedure mentioned in paragraph 10556 will be followed. If the retirement board recommends retirement and its findings are confirmed, the officer will be told that he is being retired on grounds of inefficiency arising from unsatisfactory attendance and that he has a right of appeal to the Civil Service Appeal Board.

10566. Should the officer subsequently appeal to the Civil Service Appeal Board or to an Industrial Tribunal (see paragraph 10607) and the Medical Adviser has not already considered his case, the officer will be asked to agree that this should be done. The department will need to be able either to produce the Medical Adviser's opinion or to demonstrate that the officer refused to have his case considered by the Medical Adviser.

10567-10576 unallocated.

MEDICAL GROUNDS

10577. The provisions for granting retirement on medical grounds do not apply to officers who formally retire on or after reaching their minimum retirement age and then continue to serve in a re-employed capacity, nor to officers who are due to be retired at or after age 65.

10578. If a department proposes to retire an officer for health reasons, of if an officer himself wishes to retire on grounds of ill-health, the case will be referred to the Medical Advisory Service at the earliest possible stage.

10579. If, in accordance with the advise given by the Medical Advisory Service, the department decides to retire the officer his retirement should not actually take place before the date of the retirement certificate. The department will tell the officer that he is being retired on medical grounds and give him 9 weeks notice of the date on which retirement is to take effect, unless a shorter period is mutually convenient. If the cancellation of an appointment during probationary service is in question, the period of notice will be 5 weeks. These periods of notice should be increased, where appropriate, in accordance with the rules relating to "Notice" set out in Code paragraph 10402.

10580-10584 unallocated.

Appeals against retirement, or against refusal to allow retirement on medical grounds

10585. Any officer who can furnish medical evidence in his support has the right of appeal to a medical board in either of the circumstances covered by paragraph 10578. The deicision of the board will be final and no further appeal can be allowed. An officer will be fully informed by his department of his right to appeal and acquainted in detail with the terms and conditions set out in paragraphs 10586 to 10592.

10586. The officer should normally submit his appeal and supporting evidence through his department and before he leaves the service; but exceptionally a late appeal will be considered provided he makes it with the supporting evidence within 2 months of his date of retirement and provided he has received no payment under a superannuation award, other than an interim payment in anticipation of the award of the pension (see paragraph 10587). If the officer is unfit to make the appeal himself, a close relative or friend or his staff association may appeal on his behalf during the allowed period. If the cancellation of an appointment during probationary service is in question and the person concerned or his staff association is considering an appeal, the officer may be allowed an extension of up to a further 3 weeks on the normal period of 5 weeks notice.

10587. When an appeal is under consideration, steps to attain a superannuation award are suspended and superannuation is not completed until the officer concerned or his staff association notifies the department that it does not intend to appeal or, if an appeal is made, that the appeal is settled. If necessary, however, an interim payment in anticipation of a superannuation award may be made.

10588. The period of notice of retirement on medical grounds should afford adequate time for the officer or his staff association to decide whether there are grounds for an appeal. Beyond this period, the officer will not be allowed to remain at work or to resume duty, nor will sickness pay be continued, pending the outcome of an appeal.

10589. The case, together with the supporting medical evidence, will be referred to the Medical Adviser. If the evidence does not warrant a revision of the previous opinion, the Medical Adviser will then decide whether there is a prima facie case for reference to a medical board.

10590. If it is decided that there is a prima facie case, the appellant will not be required to pay any part of the expense of the board. But if the decision is that there is no prima facie case, and the appellant wishes nevertheless to continue with his appeal, he will be allowed access to the board provided he lodges a sum of £5 with his department. This fee will be returned if the appeal succeeds; if it fails, the money will be appropriated against the cost of the board.

10591. The Medical Adviser will make arrangements for convening the board and for presenting the case to them.

10592. An officer summoned to attend a medical board may claim travelling and subsistence expenses as if on official business.

10593-10597 unallocated.

Appeals by staff associations

10598. If the staff association so desires, and the officer concerned consents, a copy of his sickness record and the medical reasons for retirement as recorded in the retiring certificate may be sent in strict confidence to the headquarters of the staff association. In addition, the Medical Adviser will be prepared, subject to the consent of the officer concerned, to discuss the case with a headquarters officer of the staff association on the understanding that the content of the discussion is treated in strict confidence and not revealed to the officer concerned.

10599-10608 unallocated.

APPEALS TO AN INDUSTRIAL TRIBUNAL

10609. Notwithstanding the arrangements which exist for staff under notice of dismissal or premature retirement (other than under the medical retirement procedures described in paragraphs 10578 to 10598) to appeal to the Civil Service Appeal Board, an officer may exercise his legal right to appeal to an Industrial Tribunal.

10610-10639 unallocated.

References

Introduction

1. E.G.A. Armstrong, *Industrial Relations: An Introduction* (London: George Harrap and Co., 1969), p.70-77.

2. An important exception in this regard is Martin Robert Godine, *The Labour Problem in the Public Service* (Cambridge, Mass.: Harvard University Press, 1951), esp. p.21-26.

3. M.J. Fores and J.B. Heath, 'The Fulton Report: Job Evaluation and the Pay Structure', *Public Administration*, vol. 48, 1970, p.22.

4. *Report of the Royal Commission on Equal Pay, 1944-46*, Cmnd 6937, p.171-4.

5. *Report of the Royal Commission on the Civil Service, 1953-55*, Cmnd 9613, para.146, p.39.

6. *Working Conditions in the Civil Service* (London: HMSO, 1943), p.4.

7. Quoted in Leonard D. White, *Whitley Councils in the British Civil Service* (Chicago: University of Chicago Press, 1933), p.160.

8. E.H. Phelps Brown, *The Growth of British Industrial Relations* (London: Macmillan, 1959), p.355.

9. *Policies for Life at Work* (OECD: Paris, 1977), p.69.

10. *Industrial Relations Review and Report*, no.81, June 1974, p.8-11.

11. K.W. Wedderburn, *The Worker and the Law*, 2nd edn. (Harmondsworth: Penguin, 1971), p.70.

12. *Ibid.*, p.141.

13. Quoted in Hilda R. Kahn, *Salaries in the Public Services in England and Wales* (London: George Allen and Unwin, 1962), p.364.

Chapter 1

1. M.A. Pearn, 'Monitoring Equal Opportunity in the Civil Service: A Review of a Report by the Tavistock Institute', Runnymeade Trust Working Paper 3/79, March 1979, p.2.

2. David J. Smith, *Racial Disadvantage in Employment*, PEP, No. 544, London, 1974, p.14.

3. See Anthony Lester and Geoffrey Bindman, *Race and Law* (Harmondsworth: Penguin, 1972), p.205-6. For a more recent discussion of this clause see *Department of Employment Gazette*, March 1979, p.230.

4. See *Employee Relations*, vol.I, no.2, 1979, p.vi.

5. See the symposium in *Industrial and Labor Relations Review*, vol.29, no.4, July 1976.

6. Quoted in the *Department of Employment Gazette*, October 1978, p.1186.

7. Extracted from 'The Quota Scheme for the Employment of Disabled People: A Discussion Document', ESA Division of MSC, 1979.

Chapter 2

1. *Royal Commission on Trade Unions and Employers' Associations, 1965-68,* Cmnd 3623 (London: HMSO, 1968), p.54.

2. See P.B. Beaumont and M.B. Gregory, 'A Consideration of the Employer Interest in Collective Bargaining Coverage in Britain', *Industrial Relations Journal,* Summer 1980.

3. Admittedly the Trade Disputes and Trade Union Act, 1927, sought to segregate civil servants into separate unions and forbade public authorities from demanding union membership of employees, but the Act was little used and in 1946 was repealed.

4. H.A. Clegg, Alan Fox and A.F. Thompson, *A History of British Trade Unions since 1889* (London: Oxford University Press, 1964), p.468-70.

5. *Ibid.*

6. David Lockwood, *The Black Coated Worker* (London: Allen and Unwin, 1958), p.75.

7. The issues and controversy surrounding the introduction of Whitley Councils in the civil service are discussed in Henry Parris, *Staff Relations in the Civil Service* (London: George Allen and Unwin for the Royal Institute of Public Administration, 1973), chapter I.

8. *Staff Relations in the Civil Service* (London: HMSO, 1949), p.3.

9. See the local government position cited by Guy Routh, 'White Collar Unions in the United Kingdom', in Adolf Sturmthal, *White Collar Trade Unions* (Urbana, Ill.: University of Illinois Press, 1967), p.187.

10. G.S. Bain and R. Price, 'Union Growth Revisited: 1948-74 in Perspective', *British Journal of Industrial Relations,* November 1976, Table 2, p.342.

11. W.E.J. McCarthy, *The Closed Shop in Britain* (Oxford: Basil Blackwell, 1954), p.36.

12. *Memorandum by FDA, Report of the Committee on the Civil Service,* Cmnd 3638, 1968, vol.5(1), p.105.

13. G.S. Bain, *The Growth of White Collar Unionism* (London: Oxford University Press, 1970), p.124.

14. Ken Prandy, 'Professional Organizations in Great Britain', *Industrial Relations,* vol.5, October 1965, p.73.

15. R.M. Blackburn, *Union Character and Social Class* (London: Batsford, 1967).

16. Brian Bercusson, *Fair Wages Resolution* (London: Mansell, 1978), p.101.

17. O. Kahn-Freund, 'Legislation through Adjudication: the Legal Aspect of Fair Wages Clauses and Recognised Conditions', *Modern Law Review,* 1948, vol.11, p.274.

18. Bercusson, *Fair Wages,* p.345.

19. *Ibid.,* p.107.

20. P.B. Beaumont and M.B. Gregory, 'The Extent of Union Organization and Collective Bargaining Coverage in Britain', University of Glasgow Discussion Paper in Economics, no.28, 1978.

Chapter 3

1. See, for example, E.N. Gladden, *Civil Services of the United Kingdom, 1855-1970* (London: Frank Cass and Co., 1967), p.146; B.V. Humphreys, *Clerical Unions in the Civil Service* (Oxford: Blackwell and Mott, 1938), p.195-8.

REFERENCES

2. *Royal Commission on Trade Unions,* p.34.

3. Sterling D. Spero, *Government as Employer* (New York: Remsen Press, 1948), p.422.

4. Quoted in White, *Whitley Councils,* p.156.

5. H.C. Debs., vol.132, col.558.

6. *Pay of Industrial Civil Servants,* National Board for Prices and Incomes Report No.18, Cmnd 3034 (London: HMSO, 1966).

7. *Pay and Conditions of Industrial Civil Servants,* National Board for Prices and Incomes Report No.146, Cmnd 4301 (London: HMSO, 1968).

8. *Royal Commission on the Civil Service, 1912-15,* Cd 6209, para.87, chapter IX.

9. Quoted in White, *Whitley Councils,* p.122.

10. *Royal Commission on the Civil Service, 1929-31,* Cmnd 3909, para.302, chapter XI.

11. *Ibid.,* para.305.

12. Quoted in White, *Whitley Councils,* p.159.

13. White, *Whitley Councils.*

14. *Royal Commission, 1929-31,* para.311, chapter XI.

15. Quoted in Parris, *Staff Relations,* p.150-1.

16. Kahn, *Salaries in the Public Services,* p.58.

17. Guy Routh, 'Civil Service Pay, 1875 to 1950', *Economica,* August 1954, vol.21, no.3.

18. *Royal Commission on the Civil Service, 1953-55,* para.99, chapter IV.

19. *Ibid.,* para.527, chapter XIII.

20. *Ibid.,* para.172, chapter IX.

21. *Ibid.,* para.134, chapter IV.

22. *Ibid.,* para.173.

23. Thomas W. Gavett, 'Comparability Wage Programs', *Monthly Labor Review,* vol. 94, September 1971.

24. Shirley B. Goldenberg, 'Public Sector Labor Relations in Canada', in *Public Sector Bargaining,* IRRA Series, Bureau of National Affairs, Washington, D.C., 1979, p.267-8.

25. See *Personnel Management,* June 1977, p.3.

26. These terms are borrowed from Sharon P. Smith, *Equal Pay in the Public Sector: Fact or Fantasy,* Industrial Relations Section, Princeton University, 1977, p.26.

27. Incomes Data Services, *Fringe Benefits,* Study No.127, London 1976.

28. Government Actuary, *Occupational Pension Schemes 1975* (London: HMSO, 1978), p.13.

29. *Ibid.,* p.99.

30. Incomes Data Services, *Incomes Data Report,* No.224, January 1976, p.23.

31. Government Actuary, *Occupational Pension Schemes,* p.59.

32. Government Actuary, *1979 Review of the Adjustment for Differences in Superannuation Benefits* (London: HMSO, 1979).

33. *The Economist,* 5 February 1977, p.89. See also *The Guardian,* 8 January 1980.

34. H.C. Debs., 20 December 1979, col.306.

35. *The Observer,* 16 March 1980.

36. *Royal Commission on the Civil Service, 1953-55,* para.145, chapter IV.
37. *Report of the Civil Service Pay Research Unit and Board Report* (London: HMSO, 1979), p.54.
38. *Incomes Data Services Brief,* no.266, October 1977, p.28.
39. *Industrial Relations Review and Report,* no.79, May 1974, p.13-14.
40. *The Times,* 6 September 1977.
41. *Royal Commission on the Civil Service, 1953-55,* para.147, chapter IV.
42. See, for example, K.D. George, R. McNabb and John Shorey, 'The Size of the Work Unit and Labour Market Behaviour', *British Journal of Industrial Relations,* July 1977, vol. XV, no.2.
43. *Report of the Civil Service Pay Research Unit,* Appendix 8, p.55.
44. Sharon P. Smith, 'Pay Differentials between Federal Government and Private Sector Workers', *Industrial and Labor Relations Review,* January 1976.
45. George L. Stenlutto, 'Federal Pay Comparability: Facts to Temper the Debate', *Monthly Labor Review,* June 1979.
46. R. Layard, D. Metcalf and S. Nickell, 'The Effect of Collective Bargaining on Relative and Absolute Wages', *British Journal of Industrial Relations,* November 1978, vol.XVI, no.3, p.290.
47. See, for example, David Winchester, 'Labour Relations in the Public Sector in the United Kingdom', in Charles M. Rehmus (ed.), *Public Employment Labor Relations: An Overview of Eleven Nations* (Ann Arbor: University of Michigan, 1975), p.74.
48. Kahn, *Salaries in the Public Services,* p.336.
49. H.C. Debs., vol.646, col.620.
50. R.J. Liddle and W.E.J. McCarthy, 'The Impact of the Prices and Incomes Board on the Reform of Collective Bargaining', *British Journal of Industrial Relations,* July 1972, vol.X, p.437.
51. A.J.H. Dean, 'Earnings in the Public and Private Sectors, 1950-1975', *National Institute Economic Review,* November 1975, no.74, p.66.
52. R.I. Hawkesworth, 'Private and Public Sector Pay', *British Journal of Industrial Relations,* November 1976, vol.XIV, p.210-11.
53. Dean, 'Earnings in the Public and Private Sectors', p.65.
54. Hawkesworth, 'Private and Public Sector Pay', p.211.
55. Dean, 'Earnings in the Public and Private Sectors', p.66.
56. Pay Board Advisory Report No.I, *Anomalies,* Cmnd 5429, 1973, p.1.
57. Civil Service Clerical Association, *CSCA Strike Policy,* 1969, p.8-9.
58. See Robert Taylor, *The Fifth Estate: Britain's Unions in the Modern World* (London: Pan, 1980), chapter 19.
59. G. Fry, 'Civil Service Salaries in the Post-Priestley Era, 1956-72', *Public Administration,* Autumn 1974, vol.52, p.325.
60. *Report of the Civil Service Pay Research Unit,* Appendix 7, p.54.
61.' See, for example, *Bank of England Quarterly Review,* June 1979.
62. Incomes Data Services, *Incomes Data Report,* No.238, August 1976, p.23.

Chapter 4

1. *Department of Employment Gazette,* February 1963.

2. Santosh Mukherjee, *Through No Fault of Their Own*, PEP, London 1973, p.20.

3. Department of Employment and Productivity, 'Dealing with Redundancies', 1968.

4. Mukherjee, *Through No Fault of Their Own*, p.194.

5. S.R. Parker et al., *Effects of the Redundancy Payments Act*, OPCS, (London: HMSO, 1971), p.50.

6. M.R. Freedland, 'Employment Protection: Redundancy Procedures and the EEC', *Industrial Law Journal*, March 1976, vol.5, no.1, p.25.

7. W.N. Daniel and Elizabeth Stilgoe, *The Impact of Employment Protection Laws*, PSI, vol.XLIV, no.577, 1978, p.11-30.

8. *Annual Report of the Civil Service Appeal Board*, 1978.

9. *Department of Employment Gazette*, June 1976, p.591.

10. See, for example, National Joint Advisory Council of the Ministry of Labour, *Dismissal Procedures* (London: HMSO, 1967).

11. *Disciplinary Procedures and Practice* (London: Institute of Personnel Management, 1979), p.52.

Chapter 5

1. See, for example, *Policies for Life at Work*.

2. *Royal Commission on Equal Pay, 1944-46*, para.516. p.171-2.

3. See P.B. Beaumont, 'The Right to Strike in the Public Sector: The Issues and Evidence', mimeo, University of Glasgow, 1980.

4. M.A. Bienfeld, *Working House in British Industry* (London: Weidenfeld and Nicolson, 1972), p.181.

5. Department of Economic Affairs, *Public Purchasing and Industrial Efficiency*, Cmnd 3291 (London: HMSO, 1967), para.2, p.3.

6. See, for example, *Incomes Data Report*, no.276, March 1978, p.2-4.

7. R.W. Bacon and W.A. Eltis, *Britain's Economic Problem: Too Few Producers* (London: Macmillan, 1976).

8. *The Times*, 18 April 1978.

9. *Sunday Times*, 18 November 1979.

10. Charles K. Rowley, 'Liberalism and Collective Choice', *National Westminster Bank Quarterly Review*, May 1979, p.20-21.

11. Beaumont, 'The Right to Strike'.

12. *Sunday Times*, 9 December 1979.

13. *Guardian*, 22 April 1980.

14. *Sunday Times*, 6 April 1980.

15. *Guardian*, 15 April 1980.

16. *Guardian*, 29 January 1980.